WINTERWISE

WINTERWISE
A Backpacker's Guide

JOHN M. DUNN

The Adirondack Mountain Club
Lake George, New York

Published by the Adirondack Mountain Club, Inc.
814 Goggins Road, Lake George, NY 12845-4117

Photographs by the author unless noted otherwise.

Library of Congress Cataloging-in-Publication Data

Dunn, John M.
   Winterwise: a backpacker's guide / John M. Dunn.
      p.   cm.
   Includes bibliographical references and index.
   ISBN 0-935272-80-1
   1. Snow camping—Equipment and supplies. 2. Backpacking—
Equipment and supplies. 3. Snow camping—Northeastern States.
4. Backpacking—Northeastern States.   I. Title.
GV198.9.D86   1995
688.7'69—dc20   95-15220
                                                                        CIP

Printed in the United States of America
10   9   8   7   6   5   4   3   2   96   97   98   99

Foreword

The faded leaves of autumn have fallen, erasing the scratchy marks of hiking trails like a coat of fresh paint. A scent of snow hangs in the air, and the summits begin to glisten with rime ice. As winter draws near and the days grow short, it is time to hang up backpacks and boots and search for a spot by the fire. Or is it?

Since the first edition of *Winterwise* in 1988, thousands of people have come to know the joys of traveling the backcountry in winter and the sport continues to grow. Winter hiking, like so much of life, is constantly changing. Whereas a winter traverse of New Hampshire's Presidential Range was once a challenge undertaken only by veterans of many seasons' experience, it can now be done as a "guided hike," for those with the desire and the money to sign on with a professional guiding service. This phenomenon of accelerated learning affects *Winterwise* in at least two obvious ways: the first is an increased demand for up-to-date knowledge, and the second, a need to remind hikers of the persistent requirement for caution. With this explosion in training programs for winter hiking, snowshoeing and backcountry skiing, there seem to be more beginners in the woods. There are also more women. Gone are the days when winter hiking was a "man's sport," its hairy, dirty practitioners found lurking around campfires gnawing on caribou hides. Another area that continues to develop rapidly is the high-tech clothing market, and while I am delighted with my new "thermoblast underwear with 30 KB of memory" (well, skip the memory....), I am dismayed to hear beginning winter hikers lament that they've had to spend thousands of dollars to get started. I think such expense may in part be the cause for the drop in enrollment of high school and college-aged hikers in some of the programs in which I'm involved. For this reason I've strengthened my emphasis on alternatives and lower-cost options.

Thus said, the second edition of *Winterwise* is still a "how-to" book on traveling the backcountry in winter. It focuses specifically on the northeastern United States but most of the information is applicable to backcountry areas anywhere. In it I have tried to provide a foundation for the beginner as well as material of interest to the expert, with the addition of some new sections such as trip planning and preparing your car for winter that were missing from the previous edition and which should further assist newcomers. *Winterwise* is not a substitute for experience and personal instruction but rather a supplement to them. By exploring a variety of materials and methods for winter backcountry travel I hope to show the reader that no one way is "the" way. What matters is developing a personal style that is flexible and adaptable to whatever situations arise.

Since fashions come and go, and equipment is continually being upgraded and improved, I have focused as much on the skills and techniques of winter backpacking and mountaineering as on the gear itself. In the first edition I intentionally minimized the use of brand names to try to limit my own personal biases, and also because I felt that what's "in" one year may not be the next. I have continued with this philosophy, but in a few instances where there was really only one good brand of a certain piece of equipment, I weakened. Thus you may see a few more trademarks this time. It is still true, however, that knowledge and ability, not the make of a certain tent or the type of mittens one wears, are the true marks of an accomplished winter backpacker.

Over the years I have had the good fortune to learn about winter hiking and skiing from a number of excellent teachers, all of whom have emphasized two major principles: be safe and have fun. Safety is something that most of us naturally think of, and to which a large part of this book is devoted, but we mustn't forget the fun of it all. Notice the beauty of a spruce bough sweeping away the snow as it sways back and forth in the wind, the delight on our partners' faces at the end of a challenging day, and the satisfaction of snuggling down warm in our sleeping bags as the mercury drops. In answer to my opening question, no, it is not time to hang up those boots. It's time to look for that spruce bough, time to rediscover our wonder at the perfection of a snowflake, time to reacquaint ourselves with the glory of winter. Please join me there.

ACKNOWLEDGMENTS

This book took root in early 1987 when Laura and Guy Waterman suggested my name to the ADK Publications Committee as a possible author for their new winter hiking and camping text. Later that summer ADK Associate Director Rick Stevens and I met to discuss the book further at an appropriate location, the top of Mt. Jo in the Adirondack High Peaks, and soon the writing began.

Throughout the year it took to finish the manuscript Carmen Elliott, my original editor, provided me with continual moral support and professional assistance. She made numerous constructive suggestions while allowing me a great deal of literary freedom— a difficult balancing act! For the second edition Andrea Masters and Robin Richards took over the whip and drove me kicking and screaming into the "information age," with the incorporation of *Winterwise* onto a computer disk, and an end to my retyping three drafts, as I did with the first one.

Thanks are due also to Mrs. Anita Creager for allowing me to quote from her husband Joe's notes on winter bushwhacking; to Jim Wagner of The Mountaineer in Keene Valley, NY, for the loan of equipment for photos and for numerous technical suggestions; to Dr. William Mills in Anchorage, Alaska, for the frostbite photos; and to all who have helped me learn and enjoy the pleasures of traveling the backcountry in winter.

Contents

The Winter World

*"I am in love with this world. I have nestled lovingly in it.
I have climbed its mountains, roamed its forests, sailed its waters, crossed
its deserts, felt the sting of its frosts, the oppression of its heats, the
drench of its rains, the fury of its winds, and always have beauty and joy
waited upon my goings and comings."* —JOHN BURROUGHS

Winter is a season of lights and darks, a season where, lacking the
bright colors of the other three seasons, one becomes more attuned
to the subtleties, the patterns of nature, be it the lacy sculpting of
a snowbank by the wind, or the symmetry of a tree's naked
branches. The winter world is a wonderful one, a place where the
forests open up to expose the earth, giving rise to unusual views,
a hidden valley, or a distant peak from a new angle. The insects
that often plague the summer hiker are gone, and the trails and
woods are quieter. Let's take a closer look at some of the things
that make winter so special.

WEATHER

Weather is, after all, what makes winter "wintry," and so it stands
to reason that we as winter travelers would want to know as much
about the weather as possible. Winter weather not only alters the

appearance of the landscape dramatically and gives us some of our greatest joys, but it can also bring great sorrows. Accidents in North American Mountaineering, the annual publication of the American and Canadian Alpine Clubs, reported on 3871 mountaineering accidents in the U.S. from 1951–1990 in which weather was felt to be a major contributory cause 289 times, or about 8% of the time. Adding in the figures for exposure, which is generally related to weather, and lightning (which if that isn't weather, I don't know what is) brings the contribution of weather to accidents up to around 15%. The true percentage is probably even greater, especially in areas such as the northeastern states, where sudden storms and unusually severe and arctic mountain weather are the rule and not the exception. Conditions on the alpine peaks of the Northeast such as Marcy, Mansfield, Washington and Katahdin can be about as severe as any spot on the globe, with temperatures approaching minus 50°F and winds in excess of 100 miles per hour. In fact, as many hikers know, the fastest observed land-speed wind in the world, a ferocious gust of 231 miles per hour, was recorded on the summit of Mt. Washington in 1934.

It is often said "the mountains make their own weather," and to a large degree that's true. The major factors to consider in the formation of mountain weather are the temperature, moving air, the moisture in the air, and the way in which the mountain topography acts on all three.

Temperature

Did you ever notice how the gas escaping from a pressurized can feels cool? As a gas expands it cools, and mountain air, rising up from the valleys by day, does the same thing, due to the decreased barometric pressure as one rises in altitude. This can account for a temperature drop of as much as 3–5°F for every 1000 feet of altitude gained. For example, if it's 20°F in the parking lot at 1000 feet above sea level, on a 5000-foot summit one can expect the temperature to be about 0°F. As with any rule of thumb, however, there are always exceptions. On occasion the cooler air, being heavier (remember the hot air balloon), will sink to the valley bottoms. This is known as a "temperature inversion." In such cases it may actually be warmer on the summits than in the valleys, but this is a less-common scenario and not to be counted on. As this rising air cools, moisture within it condenses, forming clouds and precipita- ✿ tion. This is why the higher one goes, in general, the deeper the snow, except in areas where it has been blown away by the wind.

Moving Air

As the prevailing winds come sweeping across the plains and collide with the foothills, two things happen: the air mass is lifted by the slopes, and it is squeezed between the ground and the upper layers of air. This causes the wind to accelerate, just like water that's squirted through a nozzle. That's why it's usually windy on mountaintops, ridges, and in narrow gullies and gaps. Often just dropping down a few yards from a summit or ridge crest will turn a howling gale into a gentle breeze.

The direction of the wind is important to note, as a shift in the wind direction often heralds a change in the weather. In general in the Northeast, winds from the north or the west, if accompanied by fair skies, indicate continued fair weather for 24 or more hours, whereas winds from the east or the south tend to bring thickening clouds which are often followed by precipitation within 24 hours. Forecasting charts, such as shown in Table 1 (p. 15), can be helpful in the backcountry situation, although they should of course be supplemented by a professional forecast whenever possible.

The notion that moving air robs the body of heat more quickly than calm air is well known to all who venture outdoors in the winter. Since mountains, frozen lakes and open hardwoods are inherently windy places it is important to carry adequate wind protection on any winter trip. One of the hardest times to keep warm while winter hiking is when climbing a strenuous slope in a bitter cold wind, because due to the exertion the climber has a tendency to want to shed clothing and may even begin to sweat, while the wind gradually and insidiously steals away one's heat. Upon reaching a summit or ridge the hiker's heat production suddenly drops, and it is in these situations that one is often most vulnerable. In two separate accidents in the Northeastern mountains during the winter of 1993–94 three hikers/climbers died from exposure just at the top of an area of strenuous climbing.

In order to quantify this chilling effect of the wind, scientist

Paul Siple and his colleagues conducted a series of experiments in Antarctica in the 1940s to see how fast water would freeze under different conditions. The results of their experiments are the basis for the well-known "wind chill" conversion charts. These seem to give many people pleasure in being able to report a "wind chill factor" of 60 below, 80 below, and so on. I have, however, purposely avoided including a wind chill chart in this book for two reasons: they appear every winter in countless newspapers and magazines, and I have never really figured out what to do with the information contained in them. The point is that when it's windy we lose heat much more rapidly and so must make the necessary adjustments in our clothing, pace and route to avoid becoming overly chilled.

Air masses can also be lifted and cooled by the arrival of a "front." Fronts are formed where two different air masses meet, a confrontation of cold, dry air with warm, moist air. Fronts are characterized by an approaching trough of low pressure, a change in the temperature, clouds and precipitation. Although most of us don't carry actual barometers on our hikes, many of us do use altimeters, which will show an unexpected rise in elevation as the barometric pressure drops. For example, you may pitch your tent one night at 2500 feet according to your altimeter. In the morning your altimeter reads 3000 feet, an indication that the barometric pressure has dropped and that you should be on the lookout for inclement weather. Either that or your air mattress has exploded.

Moisture in the Air

One of the reasons that northeastern mountain weather tends to be so severe and unpredictable for such relatively small mountains is that the area lies right at the point where three major storm tracks intersect. Westerly storms coming across Canada, and storms from the western and southwestern U.S., tend to bring light to moderate precipitation and are responsible for the majority of the winter storms in the Adirondacks. Atlantic coastal storms, the legendary "nor'easters," on the other hand, tend to be preceded by easterly winds, and bring heavy snowfalls. These storms are fairly common in New England, much less so in New York.

In analyzing backcountry accidents in which the weather has

Table 1

Weather Forecasting Chart (November through April)

WIND	SKY	FORECAST
Calm	Clear or cumulus	No precipitation is likely for the next 24 hours.
W to N	Clear or cumulus	Fair and cold likely for at least 24 hours.
W to N Gusty	Stratocumulus	Clouds may be stubborn, but slow clearing is likely.
W to N Gusty	Flurries or squalls	Flurries or squalls should be followed by gradual clearing, with strong winds and falling temperatures, for 12–24 hours.
N to E	Thickening cirrostratus	Snow possible within 24 hours. May precede a nor'easter.
N to NE Strong or slowly increasing	Thickening altostratus	Nor'easter possible. Snow may begin in 6–18 hours. Cold and windy.
NE to E Slowly increasing	Thickening altostratus	Full nor'easter quite possible, within 6–8 hours. Slowly rising temperatures.
N to E	Clear or cirrus	Slow increase in clouds. Possible snow. Temperatures steady or rising.
E to S	Clear or cirrus	Possible precipitation within 18–36 hours. Rising temperatures likely.
E to S	Extensive altocumulus	Some precipitation possible within 12–24 hours. Rising temperatures likely.
E to S	Thickening altostratus	Precipitation possible within 6–18 hours. Rising temperatures likely.
S to SW Strong or increasing	Extensive altocumulus or thickening altostratus	Some precipitation possible within 6–18 hours, followed by clearing and colder temperatures.
S to W	Clear or cirrus	No precipitation likely for at least 12 hours. Temperatures will probably rise.

played a significant role, it soon becomes apparent it isn't so much the absolutes of cold and snow that cause most of the problems but rather sudden, unexpected changes in the weather that catch winter backpackers off guard. Being coastal mountains, the northeastern peaks can receive either snow or rain any month of the year. Winter rainstorms are often followed by a sudden drop in temperature which can rapidly freeze clothing and other gear and turn formerly pleasurable trails into frightening bobsled runs. Here are some examples of what can happen:

A group of four hikers clad in bluejeans, with no skis or snowshoes, hikes in to camp at an Adirondack pond in late autumn. Overnight 18 inches of snow falls. They become wet and exhausted trying to hike, and two of the members are in the early stages of hypothermia as they finally stumble out to their car.

A surprise winter rainstorm catches a party of six on a snowshoe trip in Maine's Baxter State Park. They find themselves trapped between two rivers and, unable to cross either one, need to be rescued.

Four skiers take a 30-mile tour through the rugged and isolated Mahoosuc Notch near the Maine-New Hampshire border. On the second night out the temperature drops to minus 20°F, where it stays for a week. With only single-weight touring boots and no overboots, two of the four suffer frostbite.

To Avoid Such Pitfalls

Obtain the latest and most accurate weather reports prior to your departure. If you're unsure of your group's preparedness for the expected conditions, consider bringing extra gear, scaling down your plans, or even postponing the trip until the weather improves.

Try to err on the side of bringing a little bit extra, especially on multi-day trips. Be sure you have adequate clothing and other gear for any possible weather conditions.

Be alert to changing weather conditions and *be willing to modify your route* before things become "desperate." Such flexibility of thinking is critical!

SNOW FORMATION

As the moist mountain air rises and cools, droplets of so-called "supercooled" water (because it actually gets slightly colder than 32°F before freezing) collide with particles of dust and instantly crystallize. The crystals that result are six-sided and may range from thin, delicate stars and plates to long needles and columns. These crystals may then go on to do one of three things: grow as is, coalesce into snowflakes, or become coated with more supercooled particles of water to form irregular, frozen pellets known as "graupel" (rhymes with "cow-pull").

The rate at which the snow falls is determined by the amount of moisture in the air, the temperature, and the wind. Wind blows snow over and off of the windward slopes and deposits it on leeward ones. This difference in "loading" of slopes with snow can be marked and is an important factor in avalanche formation. A good example of this can be seen in Tuckerman's Ravine on Mount Washington, where the deposited snow may reach depths of 50 to 100 feet and last well into the summer, long after the neighboring windward slopes to the west are bare.

From the time snow has fallen until it melts away in the spring, it undergoes a continual process of aging due to the forces of sun, wind, pressure from layers above, and temperature differences between the ground and the air. In general, as snow ages, the sharp, symmetrical crystals gradually lose their corners and edges and become rounder. Some weather conditions, though, can produce unique and interesting snow forms, as described below:

Corn snow is corn kernel-sized granules of ice that are formed from repeated cycles of freezing at night, then thawing by day. This typically occurs in the spring and makes for good downhill skiing, as long as one waits long enough in the day for it to soften.

Cornices are curving tongues of snow and ice that hang from ridgetops and pose a threat to climbers both above (by way of falling through) and below (as a source of avalanches). Although cornices are more common in higher ranges such as the Alps, the Andes and the Himalayas, they do occasionally form on windswept ridges in the Northeast.

Crust occurs when the surface of the snow thaws and refreezes, or when rain falls on the snow and freezes. This can create quite stable snow for climbing until fresh powder falls on top of it, at which point it can act like a giant slide and cause avalanches.

Depth hoar is a crumbly, loose type of snow that is found deep in the snowpack, where warmth from the earth has caused the bottom layers of snow to recrystallize into a "sugary," unstable mass.

Rime ice occurs when supercooled droplets of water are blown against objects such as rocks and signposts, freezing instantly and forming feathery plumes of ice that build up towards the wind (contrary to one's intuition). By observing the direction of rime ice feathers one can tell how the wind has been blowing.

Sastrugi describes the erosion of wind-packed snow into a series of ridges and waves, usually indicating a firm, stable layer.

Suncups are cuplike depressions in the surface of the snow due to melting.

Verglas is a thin, transparent coating of ice due to freezing fog, rain, or meltwater that forms on rocks, trees, etc. and can make walking and climbing very hazardous.

The Innuits have some interesting and observant terms for types of snow, such as "qamaniq," the soft, sifted snow that collects in the shadows of branches, creating the notorious "spruce traps," and "siquqtoaq," or "the snow that cuts the caribous' legs," known as suncrust to us.

As noted above, certain types of snow tend to strengthen the snowpack while others make it less stable. By digging down through the snowpack and studying the successive layers of snow one can deduce a great deal about the preceding weather conditions and the inherent strengths and weaknesses of a particular patch of snow. The ability to evaluate the snow in this way is an important tool in determining avalanche risk, which is discussed in more detail in the chapter on Safety and First Aid.

FLORA AND FAUNA

"Oh, Badger," cried the Rat, "let us in, please. It's me, Rat, and my friend Mole, and we've lost our way in the snow."
—KENNETH GRAHAME, *The Wind in the Willows*

And so Mole and the Rat stumbled in out of the cold and dark of the Wild Wood and into the cheery warmth of Badger's house. Without benefit of polypropylene longjohns, pile parkas and Gore-Tex®, plants as well as animals have adapted to winter in some remarkable ways. While many plants lie dormant under a blanket of snow, the taller trees stand out and provide the winter wanderer with a wonderful opportunity to get to know them better. Notice the beeches, for example, stubbornly holding on to their leaves while the other deciduous trees have long since let go. Regard the evergreens. The dark pigments in their needles enable them to function throughout the short, dark winter days by absorbing the maximum light; and a thick waxy coat protects them from the drying effects of the cold alpine winds.

Trees are easily identified by their branches, buds, and bark. Likewise, one can discover a lot about animals by learning to recognize their tracks. At no other time of the year are we blessed with such a legible record of an animal's presence and activities as on a calm winter day following a light dusting of snow. Even the errands of mice come alive as they scamper from hole to hole and tree to tree. Foxes on patrol can be followed, deer where they sleep, and partridges as they burst out of the snow and take to the air. Animal droppings, known as "scat," help to confirm our suspicions and give us clues to what sorts of food the animals have been eating. Follow a set of tracks for a way and you may discover a young maple stripped of its bark or a hole in the snow where a partridge exploded into flight, sweeping the tips of his wings on the ground like two tiny brooms. As the snow muffles your footsteps you will be able to move through the woods much more quietly, thus increasing your chances of spotting the animals themselves, many of whom will be easier to spot as dark forms against a backdrop of white. Some of the common birds and mammals that may be seen in a northeastern winter include:

Mouse tracks in the snow.

BIRDS
ruffed grouse (partridge)
spruce grouse ("fool hen")
barred, screech and horned owls
hairy and downy woodpeckers
nuthatches
juncos
bluejays and Canada jays
black-capped and boreal chickadees
redpolls
grosbeaks
ravens and crows

MAMMALS
white-tailed deer
moose
coyotes
foxes
snowshoe rabbits and
   hares
shrews and deer mice

In addition to the obvious insulating qualities of feathers and fur, there are a number of fascinating physiological and behavioral mechanisms that allow these hearty creatures to survive subzero nights. Chickadees, for example, can shiver away in their sleep without missing a wink as a way of producing extra heat. Other animals simply allow their bodies to cool off by as much as 40-50°F below normal (the equivalent of a person cooling to about 50°F!) and recover quite easily.

Indeed, observing and learning about how other beings adapt to the winter not only increases our enjoyment of the backcountry but it also reminds us "tough" winter hikers of what truly fragile creatures we are!

For further reading on winter biology see the bibliography at the end of this book.

PRESERVING THE WINTER ENVIRONMENT

"The spirit of wilderness can be threatened from many sources — development speculators, unrestrained economic exploitation, tourist mania, overuse by thoughtless hikers, needless restrictions by wilderness managers, and others. Recreation itself can be just another form of exploitation — or it can be undertaken in a spirit of stewardship of the land. The choice is ours."

—LAURA AND GUY WATERMAN, Backwoods Ethics

We think of snow as a magical blanket that cleanses and purifies all that it touches. True, snow does protect the ground somewhat from our tromping boot soles, but it also leaves a record of our passage for those who follow behind. Whatever it might cover up temporarily comes back to haunt us in springtime.

In addition to one's normal summertime practices of clean camping and hiking, there are certain environmental concerns that are especially relevant to winter outings. For example, boots aren't the only trail eroders. The next time you take a summer hike in a popular area, look closely at the rocks in the trail. Notice dozens of fine parallel scratches heading the length of the trail? These weren't all caused by a recent glaciation; many were made by crampon points. And if crampons can do that to rocks, think how they must be digging up the soil around those rocks! Not to mention what happens when a winter hiker wearing crampons wanders off the trail on the summit cone of Mount Marcy or Washington or any of the other alpine peaks, and stomps on an

Moose prefer the bark of young maples.

ice-crusted patch of Diapensia. Ice axes and skis, especially metal-edged ones, can do damage, too.

The point is, backcountry users must learn to tread softly in all seasons. In fact, during the springtime "mud season" and other periods of heavy thaw when the ground is particularly susceptible to erosion, it's best to stay out of the woods altogether. There was a time in the United States when by forsaking the trails and heading off into the "untrampled wilderness" the climber or backpacker could be pretty well certain of not finding a trace of human disturbance. In recent years, however, such "bushwhacking" has become increasingly popular, to the point where many of the trailless peaks, waterfalls, and other popular destinations are littered with bits of surveyor's tape put up by well-intentioned parties who wanted to "mark out the route" for others to follow or for themselves on the return. This not only spoils the sense of adventure for those who actually enjoy the art of routefinding but also leads to the formation of unmaintained, eroded "herd paths." Better to learn the skills of winter navigation than to rely on the false sense of security such "red ragging" offers.

A popular misconception among some winter campers seems to be that snow causes things like toilet paper and charcoal from wood fires to dissolve. It does not. After "communing with Mother Nature" take an extra second and touch a match to your used T.P. Stand upwind.

Shouting, radios, tape decks, and barking dogs should all be discouraged. Speaking of dogs (which I happen to love), they can really mess up a nice set of ski tracks. If you do bring your dog out in the winter woods, please try to keep him out of the tracks, out of the way, and generally out of mischief.

Except for the sounds of the wind scolding the barren earth, winter tends to be a quiet season, which is one of the great joys of winter traveling.

First Steps

"I have laid footprints in the snow, a long line stretching back as far through stormy air as I could see, a stitchery of frosty prints on frozen ground." —GEORGE BASCOMB, "Prelude"

Since I wrote the first edition to *Winterwise* there has been a significant increase in the number of people enjoying the winter backcountry, and yet there are still those who feel the call and ask, "How do I begin?"

As with anything else, it's best to build up to winter backpacking gradually. By starting with easier day trips in late fall or early spring one can get a taste of some cold and snow without having to brave four-foot drifts and sub-zero temperatures. Ultimately the best way to learn is by doing, of course, but reading articles and books is also useful to strengthen one's base of knowledge and fill in the gaps. Experience in winter travel and camping may be gained either formally as part of a school or club, or informally with a circle of knowledgeable friends. Inexperienced winter hikers should never attempt to "go it alone." There are so many safer and more enjoyable ways to be introduced to the sport, such as the week-long Winter Mountaineering School sponsored jointly by the Adirondack and Appalachian Mountain Clubs. About one hundred students from teenagers to senior citizens complete this "Winter School" each year, learning everything from the basics of winter hiking and backpacking to leadership skills. For more information contact the Adirondack Mountain Club (ADK). There are also many excellent programs available through other local hiking clubs, colleges, national organizations like Outward Bound and the National Outdoor Leadership School (NOLS), and private hiking and climbing schools. Since I cannot acknowledge all of these schools I have intentionally avoided including an incomplete list in this book.

GROUPS

People hike in groups for social, educational, and safety reasons: we go out into the winter wilderness with other people because we enjoy their company and the feeling of working together to achieve a common goal rather than competing with them as we so often find ourselves doing in our day-to-day lives; we go with people of different experience levels so that we may teach or learn from them; and, lastly, we go in small groups for the safety in numbers. In the event of an accident where outside assistance is needed, it's best to have a group of at least four people so that one person can stay with the victim while two others head out for help. Although this rule is not always followed on short day trips of minor difficulty, any group smaller than four should be experienced, properly equipped, and should understand the potential dangers. On the other hand, too large a group will be slower, more difficult to keep together, and more destructive to the environment in terms of waste, noise and erosion. A group size of ten is the maximum recommended by the U.S. Forest Service, the Scouts, and the New York State Department of Environmental Conservation, among others.

The care with which one picks a team of companions for a winter trip generally varies in proportion to the length and difficulty of the trip. For a ski tour around the local golf course just about anyone would do, whereas for a major alpine or arctic expedition one's choice of partners is critical. Many otherwise promising expeditions have failed for lack of group cooperation and cohesiveness. It is not only important to pick people one *likes*, but also with similar goals and approaches. I once went on a two-week backpack in a remote region of the northern Cascades with a group of very good friends, but when we got to our base camp after three days of strenuous bushwhacking, it turned out that we all really had different objectives in mind! Different groups function differently, of course, but in most situations there are some basic unwritten (until now) rules of "group hiking etiquette." These include:

1. Stay together. A good way to ensure this is for each member of the group to keep the person *behind* him or her in sight. This prevents people from pulling away from slower companions. Splitting up groups has been seen time and time again to result in lost or injured hikers.
2. Travel at the pace of the *slowest* member. Sometimes this works best by having the stronger members in front breaking trail, but it is often the case that keeping the slower members of the party in the rear demoralizes them and makes them even slower. Allowing them to take the lead gives them a chance to share in the fun of routefinding and a view other than some faster hiker's backside. This often has the effect of speeding them up to the point where the previously faster hikers start having trouble keeping up! This leads to number three:
3. Rotate the lead often, not only to share the work of routefinding and trailbreaking, but also the fun of it.
4. Step to the side of the trail to make adjustments. When one person in the group has to stop to adjust a piece of clothing, tighten a binding, take a drink of water or whatever (provided it's not a prolonged stop), that person should step aside, allowing the others to pass by and not interrupt the flow of the group. This way the group can maintain its pace and not get spread too far apart.
5. Pull over and let others pass. When groups meet on the trail heading in opposite directions, it is generally polite for one group to pull over and let the others pass. Likewise, if a faster group catches a slower one heading in the same direction, the slower group should pull over as soon as they can, and wait a minute or two before resuming travel, so as not to follow right on the heels of the others. There is little so frustrating as having two hiking groups going at similar rates "leapfrogging" one another as first one, then the other stops for clothing changes, lunch, etc. If you pass another group, please move along and don't stop in front of them five minutes down the trail!

Being a follower in a group, while perhaps not as demanding as being the leader, does carry with it certain responsibilities. Among them are listening to the leader and being open and honest with your own thoughts and feelings, letting the leader know how you are doing, and keeping an eye on your surroundings (the weather, the trail, etc.) and your companions. In short, the followers should try to make all the observations the leader does and provide as much data to the leader as they can, but then allow the leader the ultimate decision-making power when it is needed.

LEADERS AND LEADERSHIP

In most groups it is customary to have a leader, although many small, close-knit parties go without one and make decisions democratically. There are times, however, when even a small group is unable to reach a consensus. In these cases the need for a leader becomes frustratingly evident. Before a trip even starts the leader's work begins, selecting party members, deciding on the final itinerary, planning meals, choosing what individual and group gear will need to be brought, and making the final transportation and rendezvous plans. Ideally the leader is someone who can see "the big picture" by understanding both the human and the physical elements that affect the party's progress; who can anticipate changes and make thoughtful decisions as needed; and who will see to it that the proper actions are carried out. In short the leader's goal, according to Dan Allen in his very informative booklet *Don't Die on the Mountain*, is to "bring everyone back as safely and contented as possible." The leader need not necessarily be the physically strongest member of the party, but it is a challenging role requiring not only knowledge, experience and judgement, but also the support of everyone else in the group. Many leaders grow into the role gradually by first learning the skills of winter travel and how to be good followers, then perhaps by "co-leading" trips with a more experienced partner, and finally by leading trips of increasing complexity. Some organizations offer courses specifically on leading in winter, which can help accelerate the process somewhat; but it is still essential for the would-be winter leader to have a solid background in winter backcountry skills before attempting to lead others.

All of the above-listed qualities go for naught if the leader can't communicate to the rest of the party. This begins by making his or her expectations clear before the trip even starts, and providing information to the group about the itinerary, difficulty of the trip, equipment required and so on. An orientation meeting prior to the trip, or even a get-acquainted hike, if it is to be a multi-day trip, is advisable, to allow party members to share their goals and expectations, and clear up any questions or misunderstandings that may have arisen. Once out on the trail the leader must be able to anticipate problems before they happen and recognize subtle difficulties different members of the party may be having. The leader should involve the group in decision-making when possible and encourage members to work together and help one another out. Giving encouragement and feedback, both during the trip and after, is another task for the leader. In more formal groups it is good to have a short "debriefing" after each trip, to discuss how things went, things that went well in addition to those that did not.

One of the most impressive modern examples of leadership is that of Sir Ernest Shackleton who, in Antarctica in 1915, led his party of 28 men away from their sinking ship and over hundreds of miles of pack ice, then in an open sailboat crossed 700 miles of treacherous seas and finally traversed a glaciated mountain range to reach safety. The entire expedition lasted 19 months, during which time not a single man was lost. Now there's an example to which leaders everywhere might aspire.

FAMILIES AND CHILDREN

Winter hiking and backcountry skiing can be a wonderful experience for people of all ages. When I was a caretaker at a remote backcountry lodge in the White Mountains of New Hampshire, I saw a number of children as young as four who skied the six miles in with their parents, as well as infants of five months who rode in on sleds. Winter adventures for children can be a wonderful way to experience the natural world, and a valuable lesson in self-sufficiency which will stand them in good stead no matter

CARL E. HEILMAN II

A sled or pulk gets the whole family involved.

what they go on to do as adults, even politics. Such activities are not risk-free, however, and a few words of caution are in order. Remember, you will need plenty of extra energy to care for your children without being able to worry about your own well-being very much, so you should not attempt any trips with which you, as an adult, would not be totally comfortable. Start your children out even more gradually than you might yourself, with half-day trips or shorter, then build up. Teaming up with other families is a good way of sharing the difficulties for the parents and sharing the fun for the kids. Take your time to observe things along the way—for a child a tree full of holes made by a pileated woodpecker may be a thousand times more interesting than a summit or distant view. Keep it flexible so you can take advantage of the shows nature offers—the best ones may not follow a predictable schedule. Although a healthy child is quite resistant to cold, there are a number of special considerations one should make when bringing children on winter hiking trips. For one thing, children may not tell you when they're too hot or too cold, so you must make certain their clothing is adequate. Once on the trail, check them often. If they're riding in a backpack or sled, remember that they won't be generating the same sort of heat as you will, and so will need correspondingly more insulation. Wet diapers, like any wet article of clothing, can draw off considerable heat, so check frequently for this. It is also a sign that your child is adequately hydrated. To keep childrens' faces warm, a layer of protective gel can be applied, or a child-sized facemask. Bright sunlight on snow is also a hazard to small ones, so be sure to pack the necessary sunglasses or goggles. As wonderful as it can be to be tucked snug in your tent, surrounded by loved ones, keep in mind that no matter how much you may love winter backpacking, that doesn't mean your family will. All you can do is introduce them to the sport, and what happens next is largely up to them. In spite of these potential problems, helping a loved one discover the joys of exploring the outdoors in winter enables you to relive some of your own first experiences, and seeing this fascinating new world through the eyes of another could be one of the most exciting and rewarding journeys you will ever take.

GETTING READY

Your Body

Before starting any new form of exercise one should be in good general health. Any person who is sedentary or at high risk for heart disease should consult a physician before embarking on a new exercise program.

WHY CONDITION?

Come the first heavy snow of winter, old-time fur trappers would drag their long, wooden snowshoes down from the attic and hike their 20-or-so-mile traplines with nary a thought to conditioning. Most were in excellent shape generally, but because their shin muscles weren't used to the strain of the weight of snowshoes plus snow, many of them developed a painful inflammation similar to the athlete's "shin splints." The trappers had a remedy for the problem, though—they found that the pain disappeared if they seared the skin on their shins with a red hot poker! If such an idea appeals to you, skip the following chapter; but if you'd rather enjoy winter backpacking with maximum ease and minimum pain, read on.

WHAT IS CONDITIONING?

Conditioning is a way of getting in shape for a given activity, and it is absolutely necessary for anyone preparing for a season of winter hiking and camping. It includes: maximizing cardiovascular fitness and stamina, strengthening certain muscle groups, and improving flexibility.

Cardiovascular fitness and stamina are what keep us going all day with heavy packs in heavy snows. This is due to the ability of the heart and lungs to bring nutrients to the muscles and in turn the muscles' ability to make use of them. The best exercises to increase fitness and stamina involve rhythmic, repetitive movements of large muscle groups against a relatively small resistance. Such exercises increase the body's demand for oxygen and hence are often referred to as "aerobic." Good aerobic exercises for winter backpacking include walking briskly (especially up hills or stairs, or around the neighborhood with a backpack on), hiking, jogging or running, swimming, cycling, rowing, jumping rope, skating, and crosscountry skiing. For backpacking, however, there is really nothing as good as backpacking itself. Spending an hour or two per day on the local stair-climbing machine is useful, but it's a far cry from carrying a heavy pack uphill all day. Certain other forms of exercise such as weightlifting, isometrics, shoveling, push-ups and sit-ups require a rather sustained movement against much higher resistance, and these "anaerobic" type activities, although of use for muscle building, aren't as good for the heart and lungs as the more aerobic exercises.

The demands of chugging up a 30° incline with a 30-pound pack in 30 inches of powder put a considerable stress on certain body parts in addition to the heart and lungs, most noticeably the thigh and calf muscles, shoulders and arms, and the back and trunk. In trying to strengthen these muscle groups it's important to understand that muscles strengthen faster than tendons and ligaments, and so one must progress slowly to avoid nagging overuse injuries like tendinitis. One of the most common errors in doing muscle building exercises is the tendency to think "It doesn't hurt now, so it must be all right," and to do too much too soon. DON'T STRAIN—it may feel fine at first, but in a few weeks it may catch up with you.

Strengthening
The photos on pages 34–35 illustrate some simple strengthening exercises one can do with a minimum of space and equipment.

Stretching
Stretching aims at improving flexibility and making the body move more efficiently. Winter clothing inhibits movement enough without being compounded by over-tight muscles and tendons. Due to the colder temperatures and the paraphernalia attached to one's feet in the winter, muscle strains, especially of the thigh and groin muscles, seem to be more common than in summer. Stretching can also decrease the number of injuries caused from overdoing it or as the result of falls. The stretch should be slow and gentle, gradually lengthening the muscle group to the point where a warm, pulling

sensation occurs, not pain; that position should be held for ten seconds or more. Forget about any bouncing, violent stretches you may have learned earlier; these are very likely to cause injuries. The photos on pages 37–39 illustrate several stretches that are good for winter hikers and climbers.

Strengthening exercises: (a) Sideways leg raises help tone up those snowshoeing muscles. (b) Plain old pushups are simple and good for the arms, shoulders, and trunk muscles.

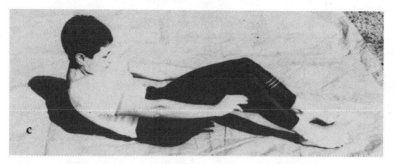

(c) Sit-ups should always be done with bent knees to prevent back strain.

TOTAL EXERCISE SESSION

A total exercise session should include a *warm-up period* of ten minutes or so of gentle stretching and gradually beginning the exercise; *an aerobic or anaerobic period*; and a *cool-down period* of gradually stopping the exercise followed by ten to fifteen minutes of loosening and stretching. This same approach can and should be used on all winter hikes or ski trips. To benefit from aerobic exercise, the sessions must be of an adequate intensity, duration and frequency but not so much as to cause injuries. Most experts agree that a reasonable intensity of exercise can be estimated by achieving and maintaining what's known as an individual's target heart rate (THR). This represents 60-80% of a person's maximum heart rate (MHR), which is estimated based on the age of the person.

A rough way of calculating your THR is to subtract your age in years from 220 to obtain your MHR, and then take 60–80% of that; for example, the estimated MHR for a 40-year-old would be 220 − 40 = 180 beats per minute, and the THR would then be 60–80% of that, or between 108 and 144 beats per minute (see also Table 2, [p. 36]). This is the pulse range the average 40-year-old should aim for during aerobic exercise to obtain a good "training effect." Note, however, that it is certainly possible to benefit from milder levels of exercise, and in recent years the usefulness of the target heart rate has been called into question by some experts. The duration of exercise should probably be 20 to 30 minutes per session initially, at a frequency of three to five times per week. This can be gradually increased if desired, ideally no more rapidly than

Table 2
Target Heart Rates for Aerobic Exercise

AGE	MHR	60%	70%	80%
20	200	120	140	160
30	190	114	133	152
40	180	108	126	144
50	170	102	119	136
60	160	96	112	128
70	150	90	105	120
80	140	84	98	112

at two- to three-week intervals. To progress much faster than this runs the risk of producing "overuse" iniuries. It should be pointed out, however, that to go out and hike all day long, one will have to work up to at least some full days in the field. In other words, don't expect to go easily from one-hour gym sessions to full days of backpacking, no matter how vigorous the sessions. To build stamina it is necessary to do some longer sessions, usually at least once a week. A good example of this is the marathon runner. To build up to running 26 miles at a stretch it isn't necessary to run 26 miles every day, or even 20, but it is a good idea to work up to a longer run (say 15–20 miles) every week or so.

Make no mistake: winter backpacking is a strenuous sport. But with proper conditioning, including attention to stretching, strengthening, and stamina, you can get ready for it gradually, avoid injuries, and leave the hot poker by the fire where it belongs.

Stretching exercises. (a) Groin stretch—lean forward to increase the stretch. (b) Gluteal (buttock) muscle stretch. (c) Hamstring stretch. Note position of the left leg, which is easier on the knee than the traditional "hurdle" position. (d) Calf muscle stretch using stairway. (e) This position stretches both the hamstrings and the groin muscles, as well as the calf if the foot is pulled back.

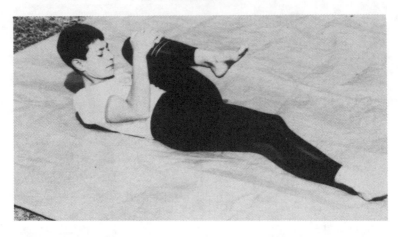

Stretching exercises, continued. (f) The back needs stretching too. Pull one or both knees to your chest and hold for ten seconds. (g) Press-up to help restore your back's natural arch.

Stretching exercises, continued. (h) Back arching from a standing position—a good thing to do after taking off that hundred-pound pack! (i, j) Make use of your ski poles to loosen your shoulders before starting a ski.

Your Car

Having a perfectly tuned body is useless if you can't even get to the trailhead. For most of us these days that means travel by car. Actually, the more common problems arise when one returns from a hike, tired, maybe a little wet, starting to cool down, and hops in the car, turns the key, and rrr!...rrr!...rr!..r!..r... It won't start! To keep your car in shape for your winter adventures, consider the following:

1. Tune it up at least once a year, preferably in the fall.
2. Keep the battery well-serviced, replace it ahead of time, and be sure it's rated for very cold-weather starts. Carry a good set of jumper cables, too, just in case, and back into any tight parking spots.
3. Be sure your antifreeze is adequate (minus 40°F in New England).
4. Use a lighter-weight oil in the winter, e.g. 5W-30 (check your owner's manual).
5. Always keep your tank at least ¼ full to decrease moisture build-up in the gas tank, and use dry gas liberally, especially before parking it for a long winter's night.

Two other areas to consider in addition to cold-weather starts, are visibility and traction. Be sure to have plenty of windshield washer fluid on board and a good scraper or two. To keep your car moving forward invest in a good set of snow tires, carry a shovel, some sand or traction pads, tire chains, a tow rope or chain, and consider four-wheel drive if you are going to be doing a lot of driving in snowy regions.

Planning Your Trip

Okay, now that you've gotten in shape, tuned up your car, and covered the basics, where do you go and what do you do? To start out planning a trip I like to use the journalist's approach: consider the "Five ?'s," i.e. the Who, What, When, Where, and How.

Who means picking your partners, and is covered in the section on Groups. Remember that for a trip of any more than a weekend, most people need at least several weeks' to months' warning, to arrange time off from work, etc. To a certain extent, the type of trip being planned will affect the number and types of people invited, although it is common for a group of friends to decide to go on a trip together before they know where they're going.

What you will do, i.e., the type of trip (snowshoeing vs. skiing, day trip vs. several week expedition, etc.) depends on the interests and resources of the group. Remember to scale down your plans for the winter. If the going is rough, (e.g., heavy snows, steep climbing, etc.) even five miles may be a big day. While leading a group on a five-day winter backpack one year I planned on a fairly easy first day: five miles of very moderate uphill. As it turned out it snowed all day long making the party wet and the snowshoeing strenuous, and we were lucky to drag into camp by dusk. The following day, with nearly two feet of new snow, we were only able to make two and a half miles. Another winter it took myself and a group of my friends four attempts to reach the summit of a 14,000 foot peak in Colorado. The point is that things are much more difficult in winter, and it is essential to plan trips accordingly, along with contingency plans. Whereas in summer, for example, one can generally count on being able to complete a traverse of New Hampshire's Presidential Range, in winter this is far from a given. Due to snow conditions, high winds, storms and heavy packs, the winter success ratio on this trip is closer to one trip in three.

When to go on a winter trip is usually easy. Winter seems to fly by so fast we get in our trips whenever we can. "Early winter" (unofficially November and December in the Northeast) suffers, however, from the problems of short days and thin snow cover. "Mid-winter" (January and February) the snows are usually better and the days a little longer, but the temperatures can be brutal. "Late winter" (March and April) is generally a lovely time of the year, with longer days, milder temperatures, and a thick blanket of snow for skiing and snowshoeing.

Where then, to go, is limited only by your time, money, and imagination. Usually the first two, for most of us. Look at maps of the country (or world). Talk to friends who've done interesting trips. Go to lectures and slide shows. Read outdoor, travel and adventure magazines. If your time and budget are small, look in your own area. Many popular places in summer are almost deserted in winter. I have skied or hiked by a popular summer camping area on Vermont's Long Trail about six times in the past two winters, and I have never seen anyone there.

At last: you know where you want to go, what you want to do, who your companions will be, and when you will do it. So, *how* are you going to pull it all off? First, be sure you have the time free, from work, meetings, family obligations, etc. Then send for any permits and reservations (backcountry or lodging) you will need. While you're waiting for those to arrive, make a detailed list of all the food and gear you'll require (see Appendix). If more gear needs to be bought, do it early—fit it and test it out well beforehand. Also, old gear should also be checked for repairs that are needed, and to be sure it is fitted properly. (How about those crampons you readjusted last spring to fit on your lighter boots? How about that pack your six-foot-eight brother-in-law borrowed?) Buy all your food, pack it, and be sure it all fits in your pack with your gear. If the trip involves significant travel, hotel or motel lodging en route, entry fees, etc., make a budget. Include any "group gear" that needs to be purchased, such as stove fuel, ropes, playing cards, etc.

When all this is done, go over it again. There is little so frustrating as arriving at your destination to find the cabins are all reserved, or the trail has been moved, or you forgot some critical piece of equipment. But try not to think of planning as a chore. As you tighten those snowshoe bindings or package that food, imagine yourself away in the wilderness on a glorious day with the sun shining down on two feet of fresh, glistening snow. It's all part of the experience.

WINTER CAMPING REGULATIONS

Rules for camping vary tremendously from area to area, and it is the responsibility of the camper to find out beforehand just what they are. Not only are improper camping practices bad for the environment, but many of them also carry significant penalties, including fairly sizeable fines, public floggings, and so on.

To detail the camping regulations for the entire Northeast would require a book in itself; but here are the general guidelines for a number of the major northeastern hiking and camping areas to give the winter camper some idea of what to expect. For specific information contact the Forest Service, park officials, hiking clubs or other reputable organizations in the area in question well in advance of making the trip. Some of their telephone numbers and addresses are included below.

The Adirondack Park, the largest single chunk of wildlands in the Northeast, covers an area roughly the size of the state of Vermont (or New Hampshire) and is a curious blend of public and private lands. There are many three-sided lean-tos available on a first-come, first-served basis, and many established campsites. No camping or fire permits are required except for groups of ten or more people. Throughout the park there is no camping within 150 feet of any trail, stream or other water source except at designated campsites. There is also no camping above 4000 feet in elevation between April 30th and December 1st, which means that winter campers technically may camp higher than this, but it is not recommended due to the fragility of the alpine environment and the severity of the weather conditions at these heights. For further information one should contact either the New York State Department of Environmental Conservation (DEC) Forest Ranger in the area where one is intending to camp, the DEC headquarters in Ray Brook, N.Y. (tel. 518-897-1200), or the Adirondack Mountain Club (ADK).

Another major hiking and camping area, the White Mountains of New Hampshire, is made up largely of the White Mountain National Forest (WMNF), part of which extends into the western part of Maine. The Appalachian Mountain Club (AMC) operates two backcountry "huts" several miles from the road throughout the winter season where winter hikers and skiers may stay in a four-sided, minimally-heated building and use hut pots, pans and propane stoves to prepare their own food. The Randolph Mountain Club (RMC) maintains several facilities in the northern Presidential Range, including one (Gray Knob) that is also partially heated and has a caretaker in residence. As in the Adirondacks, there are also a number of lean-tos (usually called shelters) available, and many other areas where one may pitch a tent, although it is here that things become a bit more complicated. Within the WMNF there are several nationally designated "wilderness areas" that are intended to be preserved in as near a primitive state as possible, and for that reason all of the shelters and other man-made structures are being gradually removed. Two of these areas, the Dry River and Great Gulf Wilderness areas, cover sizeable areas of land in and around the popular Presidential Range (it's the range that is popular, not necessarily all the presidents!), and the status of camping in these areas has changed a number of times over the past several years. Currently it is legal to camp above treeline in New Hampshire only in certain areas, and only when there is at least *two feet of snow*. It is a good idea to double check this with the Forest Service before heading out, as hiker impact may cause this to change.

There are a number of other heavily-used areas that, while not actually "wilderness areas," have been designated "Forest Protection Areas" by the Forest Service. In these areas camping and wood or charcoal fires are not allowed within 200 feet of trails or a quarter mile of shelters and other popular spots, except in designated sites. There are also three major state parks in the WMNF (Crawford Notch, Mt. Washington and Franconia Notch) in which there is no camping except in designated areas. Fire permits are required on WMNF lands only when there is no snow on the ground. Further information can be obtained from the district rangers in the towns of Plymouth, Bethlehem, Conway, and Gorham, NH; from the WMNF Office in Laconia (tel. 603-528-8721); or from the AMC at Pinkham Notch Camp, Gorham, NH 03581 (tel. 603-466-2727). Ask for a "Backcountry Camping Rules" brochure, which will highlight all of the various areas mentioned. Simple, eh?

Perhaps even more complex is the situation in Maine where there is some national forest, a national park (Acadia), a major state park (Baxter), and significant areas of northern wilderness, some of which is "organized" and some of which is "unorganized." There is a very good publication called "Forest Campsites," which is available from the Maine Forest Service, State Office Building, Augusta, ME 04330, and which details some of the rules and regulations. Other good sources include the AMC's *Maine Mountain Guide* (see references), an organization called North Maine Woods, Box 113, Bangor, ME 04401, which publishes a guide map of the organized and unorganized territories with the latest regulations, and the Paper Industry Information Office, 133 State Street, Augusta, ME 04330 (tel. 207-622-3166). In Baxter State Park the rules are quite strict and precise. All camping, climbing and hiking requires a special use permit from the Park Authority,

Table 3
Sources of Winter Camping Regulations

NEW YORK
Adirondacks • Catskills
Sources: Department of Environmental Conservation, Ray Brook, NY 12977
(518) 897-1200

Adirondack Mountain Club
814 Goggins Road, Lake George, NY 12845
(518) 668-4447

NEW HAMPSHIRE
White Mountain National Forest
Sources: Regional rangers in Plymouth, Bethlehem, Conway, and
Gorham, NH

Forest Supervisor, Laconia, NH
(603) 528-8721

Appalachian Mountain Club, Pinkham Notch Camp, NH
(603) 466-2727

MAINE
Acadia National Park
Source: Bar Harbor Park Headquarters
(207) 288-3338

Baxter State Park
Source: Supervisor, BSP, Millinocket, ME 04462

White Mountain National Forest
Source: see New Hampshire above

Northern Territories
Sources: North Maine Woods, Box 113, Bangor, ME 04401

The Paper Industry Information Office
133 State Street, Augusta, ME 04330
(207) 622-3166

VERMONT
General
Source: The Green Mountain Club Inc.
Route 100, RR1, Box 650, Waterbury Ctr., VT 05677
(802) 244-7037

Green Mountain National Forest
Source: Forest Supervisor, GMNF, Box 519, Rutland, VT 05701

State Lands
Source: Department of Forests, Parks, and Recreation
Agency of Environmental Conservation
Waterbury Complex, 103 S. Main Street, Waterbury, VT 05676

which must determine that the party is adequately equipped and competent to undertake the proposed adventure. Applications must be submitted to the Millinocket Office of the Authority *at least four weeks in advance*. A complete copy of the rules and regulations is available from the Supervisor, Baxter State Park, Millinocket Office, Millinocket, ME 04462. Information on camping in Acadia National Park may be obtained from the Bar Harbor Park Headquarters (tel. 207-288-3338).

Vermont hiking areas, like the Adirondacks, are a patchwork of public (State Forests, Green Mountain National Forest) and private lands. On the private lands along the Long Trail, camping is permitted only at shelters, whereas in the Green Mountain National Forest "dispersed" camping and fires are permitted at the hiker's discretion. On state land camping is allowed in areas designated for primitive "tent" camping, which is basically any area below 2500 feet, 200 feet from a trail or boundary line, and 100 feet from any stream or body of water.

By now you should be getting a good idea of how complicated it all is. The best advice I can give is to find out as much as you can before you go. Never start up an unknown trail with the intention of finding a campsite "somewhere up there." Just recently (in January) I ran into a nice couple from Pennsylvania who asked me where the trailhead to Mt. Mansfield was, then announced that they planned to camp on the summit! Not only may this type of approach turn out to be impractical and possibly unsafe, it may also be illegal (in the case I mentioned all three were true!).

Table 3 (p. 45) summarizes the different areas described above and tells how you may obtain additional information. Use it as a handy reference to keep your winter camping hassle-free!

Safety and First Aid

"But simply gaining additional factual knowledge in wilderness skills is seldom enough. Knowing how to apply this information for self-help is the key to autonomy and safety."

—TIM J. SETNIKA, *Wilderness Search and Rescue*

HOW ACCIDENTS HAPPEN

It's four-o-clock at the end of a long, hard day of snowshoeing. You're descending a steep hillside toward a level spot that promises good camping. One of your companions is negotiating a narrow gully, bracing herself against her ice axe which she trails like a rudder. Suddenly her snowshoe tip catches on a hidden branch. She pitches headlong down the steepening chute. Instinctively she turns her feet downhill in an attempt to self-arrest, but she drops backwards over a short ledge and begins to windmill on the snow. You watch, horrified, as she disappears from sight.

Although accidents like this fortunately are fairly uncommon in the northeastern backcountry, there are nonetheless every winter a few serious cases of trauma and cold injury, some of which end fatally. On careful inspection most of these accidents turn out to have been quite easily preventable. Not only should all hikers and skiers know what to do in case of an accident but, just as importantly, they should understand how accidents happen and know what they can do to prevent them.

Hazards in mountaineering are often divided into objective and subjective risks. Objective risks are things beyond one's immediate control, such as rockfall, avalanches and sudden changes in the weather. Subjective hazards are those made by the backpacker himself, such as bringing inadequate equipment or reading the map wrong. Looking over analyses of accidents regularly printed in many mountaineering club publications, one will see over and over again that subjective hazards, such as unpreparedness in terms of equipment, experience or conditioning, and exceeding one's abilities, are major contributing factors in most backcountry accidents. Usually it's not just a single mistake that leads to the accident but a series of errors, like a domino effect.

An example: A winter hiker inadvertently leaves home without his crampons (mishap #1), which he remembers thirty miles down the road. He wisely returns to get them, but because of this error he arrives at the trailhead at 11 a.m. Because he's now behind schedule, he hurries along (#2), not eating or drinking enough, (#3) and soaking his clothing with sweat (#4). As he reaches the summit ridge he becomes mildly hypothermic due to the combination of fatigue, wet clothing, and inadequate calories. The rest of the story is easy to imagine.

Whenever that uneasy feeling arises that things just don't seem to be going right, the party must make a conscious decision to interrupt that pattern of errors and carefully work through what has happened. Ask, where are we exactly in the overall scheme of our trip? How much daylight do we have left? And, can we get back on track, or should we alter our plans? Remember that the majority of backcountry accidents happen late in the day, when people are tired and visibility is poor. Ask yourselves, "What sort of extra food and clothing do we have? What is the physical and mental condition of the group, in particular the weakest member?" Often all it takes to interrupt a potentially dangerous pattern is a minor adjustment, such as dropping down off a ridge, camping an hour earlier, or adjusting the pace. Sometimes the best decision *is* to press on. But the psychological urge to "make the summit at all costs" or some other goal can be overwhelming. The wise backcountry traveler learns to keep that desire from clouding his judgement. A French alpine guide named Cocoz told me once that the only reason he'd lived well into his seventies, still making difficult climbs, and that no one in his family during seven generations of guiding had suffered a fatal accident, was because of their philosophy that "Zee mountaine, she ees always there." In other words, when things start to go bad, remember that you can always back off and return another day.

EMERGENCY GEAR

A few extra items of equipment can make a tremendous difference in an emergency situation. Some people carry everything from inflatable splints to flare guns, while others don't even bring a band-aid. Ultimately each individual must decide just how far to go with emergency gear by choosing the most useful, yet reasonably light and compact, items in light of that person's experience and the nature of the proposed trip. Naturally one would want to bring more on a Himalayan expedition than on a two-hour ski tour in rolling farmland.

As with regular gear, emergency equipment can be broken down into food, clothing and shelter. Food is particularly important because with adequate calories one can often hike out to safety

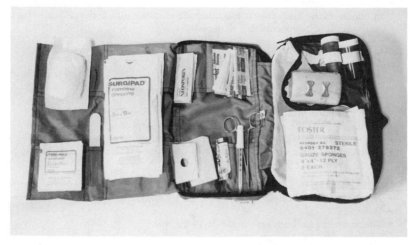

A good personal first-aid kit, containing various dressings, antibiotic ointment, moleskin, a hypothermia thermometer, tweezers, elastic bandage, and medications.

or even shiver away the night if need be, but once the body becomes depleted of energy no amount of shelter or insulation may be enough. Emergency foods should be of high calories for their weight, be easily digested, and require no preparation to eat. Dried fruits, cheeses, nuts, and candy bars are all good. One of my Vermont friends brings a small bottle of maple syrup, which packs quite a punch. The trouble is, he usually drinks it down well before any emergency! There's a reason those military emergency rations don't taste *too* good.

In addition to the usual winter clothing it's a good idea to bring along some spares, especially a spare pair of mittens, long

Table 4
Suggested First-Aid Kit Supplies

FIRST-AID MANUAL

BANDAGING/SPLINTING
- Band-aids
- Moleskin or the equivalent, for blisters
- Gauze pads: 4" x 4" most useful
- Dressing for larger wounds, e.g., 6" x 8"
- One-inch wide medical tape
- Triangular bandage for dressings, splinting, or sling
- Rolled gauze bandaging to hold 4" x 4"'s in place
- Elastic bandage (three- and four-inch wide most versatile)
- Consider additional splints (wire, metal or wooden; avoid inflatable splints in winter as they can cut off too much circulation), although they can often be improvised from available materials.

MEDICATIONS
- Antiseptic solution to cleanse wounds
- Antiseptic ointment or cream to dress wounds
- Sunscreen/block
- Water purification tablets
- Mild painkiller/anti-inflammatory, e.g., aspirin, ibuprofen
- Stronger painkiller, e.g., codeine derivatives, morphine
- An antihistamine for allergic reactions or congestion
- Consider antacids, antibiotics, and anti-diarrheal medications, depending on the group and the nature of the trip.

INSTRUMENTS
- Needle, razor, or scalpel blade for removing splinters, draining blisters, etc.
- Tweezers
- Thermometer for both fevers and hypothermia

OTHER
- Chemical hot packs

---

underwear, socks, and a hat. A lightweight pair of down or pile pants and a bulky parka can make an emergency bivouac tolerable and are great for standing around in the cold, as often happens in rescue situations.

The last category, shelter, is usually no problem on overnight trips as most of the gear (sleeping bags, tents, etc.) is being carried anyway, but the question often arises as to how much shelter a group on a day trip should carry. To bring a tent, sleeping bag and foam pad for every member of the group seems a little excessive, so many winter parties will carry one of each item per group for the hypothetical "victim." This is certainly reasonable and should be recommended, but realistically many winter day trippers, with the exception of some of the organized club or school trips, do not bring much overnight gear due to its weight and bulk. What I would suggest is that if each member of the group is carrying adequate clothing for insulation, the next most important items for emergency shelter would be protection from the wind and the ground. This can be accomplished by carrying lightweight foam pads and a large nylon bivouac sack or tent (some parties just bring the tent shell and leave the frame at home) into which the entire group can huddle for a surprising degree of comfort. Other useful items for emergency shelter include a lightweight folding or telescoping snow shovel for building mound houses or snow caves, and a knife or collapsible saw for cutting boughs for shelter (to be done only in the direst of emergencies!) or firewood. Other general items that may be of use are signalling devices such as a whistle or mirror, and fire starters (waterproof matches, candles, fire ribbon or paste), which take up little room and can be easily added to the kit. A lightweight stove takes up more room, but is great for preparing quick, hot drinks.

The first aid kit is another area of considerable individual variation and controversy. There are a number of good prepackaged kits available, but many hikers prefer to put together a kit of their own. In addition to the usual summertime supplies one might consider a low-reading "hypothermia thermometer" and several chemical "strike-to-activate" hot packs which can be used to rewarm a hypothermia victim. Table 4 (p. 50) is a checklist of suggested first-aid supplies that can be modified to individual needs and experience.

APPROACHING THE ACCIDENT VICTIM

Going back to the snowshoeing accident (p. 47), the first thing to do is take stock of the entire situation. Is anyone in immediate life-threatening danger? If, for example, your partner is teetering on the brink of a hundred foot cliff, clutching a few slippery roots, that person obviously must be attended to instantly. In so doing the rescuers must take every precaution not to place themselves in danger or increase the danger to the victim. One should approach the victim quickly but carefully from the side or below so as not to dislodge anything that might cause further harm. In general the victim should not be moved until his or her condition has been evaluated, but there are some instances in backcountry rescue where this isn't possible. When a victim must be moved every effort must be made to protect the victim's spinal cord. This means one person holds the victim's head securely in line with his body while the other rescuers log-roll him, scoop him up in their arms and move him carefully to a safe spot. All of this is done keeping the victim's spine in as close to the anatomically correct (i.e., normal) position as possible.

As anyone who has taken a basic life-support or CPR course knows, the human brain, if totally deprived of oxygen, starts to die very quickly, usually in four minutes or less. For this reason it is paramount in the initial evaluation of any accident victim to be sure that his airway is open and he is breathing spontaneously. Failure to maintain an open airway is one of the major correctable mistakes leading to death in trauma victims. You must immediately look to see if the victim's chest is moving normally, listen over the mouth and nose for the movement of air, and feel both the movement of air and the chest. Frequently the mouths and tracheas of avalanche victims are blocked with snow. Learn how to dislodge foreign material from the airway using finger sweeps of the mouth and abdominal or chest thrusts (Heimlich maneuver). These techniques are all covered in classes taught by the American Red Cross and Heart Association.

If, after opening the airway, the victim still isn't breathing spontaneously, you must know how to perform rescue breathing ("mouth-to-mouth resuscitation").

After checking the airway and breathing the next thing to do is assess the victim's circulation. Everyone should know how to feel the carotid artery pulse. If no pulse is present external chest compressions will need to be started.

Next, any major sites of bleeding must be found and compressed with a gloved hand or piece of clothing until a sterile pad can be applied. Almost all external bleeding can be halted with direct pressure, and the cases in which a tourniquet is needed are exceptionally rare. It is important to avoid direct contact with the victim's blood if at all possible, to minimize the rescuer's risk of contracting such blood-borne diseases as hepatitis or AIDS.

After attending to the airway, breathing, and circulation (the "ABC's") one can make a more detailed examination of the victim. This is a complete "head to toe" check, looking and feeling for any painful areas or deformities. It is important to go slowly and check each area carefully.

By now you should have a pretty good idea of what's wrong, and you will need to decide both on additional first-aid measures and how to get the victim out of the woods. Whether to call for additional help or try to handle everything on your own is sometimes a difficult decision. Often inexperienced groups call for "a rescue" when they in fact could get the victim out of the woods by themselves. Such "self-rescues" are not only cheaper, but in many cases they are quicker (it takes hours at best to organize and mobilize a rescue party to most places) and overall safer by not exposing many rescuers to unnecessary hazards. I have been called out for such injuries as a dislocated shoulder and possible cracked ribs. In both cases the people involved were simply encouraged to walk out on their own, and they did, in considerably more comfort than bouncing along in a litter. Another thing to consider in this day and age is that whenever a large-scale rescue occurs, there is inevitably a cry to "license hikers," charge for "rescue insurance" or even close "dangerous" areas to backcountry users. Unless we want a regimented experience, with fees and rules behind every tree, we need to learn and practice self-reliance. If, however, the situation is truly beyond your resources and you do decide you need outside help, realize that it may take hours or even overnight for someone to hike out to the road and relay the message to the proper authorities, who will then have to organize rescuers and equipment and transport them back to the trailhead to hike back in, heavily laden with rescue equipment plus their own gear.

During this interim period if you can safely begin moving the victim or assisting her to move under her own power the time saved will be worth it. If you're unable to move her at all you must settle in and stay as comfortable and warm as possible.

Often, as mentioned, with relatively minor injuries such as sprains and strains, lacerations, and upper extremity injuries, the victim may be able to walk out with assistance, which will in most cases be both quicker and more comfortable. In some cases a strong hiker can carry another by using a coil of rope or a rucksack with leg holes cut into it. If enough people are present to carry a litter, a crude but serviceable one may be made from two sturdy saplings with parkas or a rope strung between them. For skiers a good sled can be fashioned by lashing four or more skis side by side and padding them.

When outside assistance is clearly required, two or more members of the party will need to head out, with plenty of food and equipment plus careful notes on the victim's condition and exact location. Ideally the spot should be marked on a map. I remember arriving at the foot of an enormous glacial moraine in Nepal, searching for a man whose "leg had been crushed." As we started up the slope his tearful partner came stumbling down. "Where is he?" we queried. She took one look back at the several square miles of gullies and piles of loose boulders, gestured broadly and blurted, "Up there!" Two hours later we found him. When the rescue party arrives the person who is primarily in charge of the victim's medical condition should speak with the rescue team leader while everyone else gets ready to go and helps the rescue team as they are told.

SELECTED WINTER MEDICAL PROBLEMS

In addition to the usual injuries and illnesses that may befall summer hikers, winter hikers and skiers are at greater risk for cold injuries such as hypothermia and frostbite and other conditions such as snowblindness. The next few pages contain a discussion of some of the current thinking on each of these areas. For more information on backcountry medicine the reader is urged to consult the references in the back of this book and/or consider taking one of the very good backcountry medicine courses that are often available through schools, clubs, and other organizations.

Cold Injury

Although we tend to think of hypothermia and frostbite as two entirely different conditions, they are actually closely related and often occur together. By understanding how heat is produced and managed by the body we can more effectively prevent such tragedies as the two described below:

In the winter of 1982 two climbers ascended an icy gully on New Hampshire's Mount Washington. As they were climbing the weather deteriorated, blowing them well off their intended path of descent and forcing them down into a valley several miles from where they expected to be. When they were eventually found by a snowshoer who happened upon their boot tracks, one of them had suffered such severe frostbite he eventually lost both of his lower legs.

I first described the story above in 1988. In the winter and spring of 1993–94 at least five more people died in these northeastern mountains, in four separate accidents. Three were from hypothermia, one from a fall (sliding a very steep slope without an ice axe for self arrest) and in the other a person was hit by a falling block of ice. With the exception of the last one, all of these other deaths appear to have been completely preventable. In 1996 there were six deaths: two from falls, one from hypothermia and three from avalanches. Here's another, all-too-classic scenario that happened in upstate New York's Adirondacks:

Two hikers left the town of Newcomb one Thanksgiving day for a weekend backpacking trip. As they traveled through Indian Pass on their second day out, one of the pair started to falter and seemed to be having trouble with his balance. Both he and his partner assumed he was merely tired. When he could finally go no further, his partner pushed on ahead, leaving him sitting beside the trail. By the time rescuers reached him he was in the final stages of hypothermia, and as they were bringing him down to rewarm him, he died.

Hypothermia: Hypothermia is a lowering of the body's inner core temperature to 95°F (35°C) or below due to heat losses that exceed the body's ability to produce heat.

Causes: Heat is produced by metabolism of the food we eat plus our muscular activity. It is conserved by the insulation of our skin and clothing plus our bodies' ability to control blood flow so that our inner organs stay warm at the expense of allowing our extremities to cool off somewhat. Heat is lost from our bodies in four different ways. Conduction occurs from direct contact with a cold object, such as sitting on a snow-covered rock or falling in an icy stream. Convection is the loss of heat by moving air, for example a gust of wind above treeline. Heat can also radiate directly from the body surface, and lastly it can be lost by evaporation of water from one's skin or in one's expired air. Understanding these ways in which heat can be lost from the body helps us to understand why we get cold, and to be able to figure out what to do to prevent it.

Effects: The body's initial response to hypothermia is actually to speed up metabolism, as if in an attempt to resist cooling off. Below about 90°F, however, everything starts to slow down. The nervous and muscular systems are affected first, beginning with the fine motor skills such as the ability to button a shirtsleeve. Speech may be slightly slurred and, even in the early stages, judgment may be clouded. Poor judgment due to mild hypothermia has probably been a contributing factor in more backcountry acci-

Table 5
"Red Flags" for Hypothermia

* Passing out or fainting
* Confused, illogical thinking or behavior
* Unusual forgetfulness; losing or misplacing critical items
* Difficulty seeing
* Slurred speech
* Trouble with fine motor tasks
* Extreme fatigue
* Stumbling, unsteady gait
* Uncontrollable shivering
* Inability to keep fingers and toes warm

dents than we realize. In the later stages there may be gross inco-ordination, confusion, combativeness and finally, if untreated, coma and death. There are a number of cases of hypothermic hikers and climbers becoming so confused and combative that they had to be forced to descend or even had to be abandoned. Table 5 (p. 56) is a list of some of the "red flags" that may signal hypothermia.

In the most severe situations, the circulatory and respiratory systems are depressed to the point where there may even be no detectable breathing or pulse. In fact there are reports of suppos-edly dead patients "coming to life" on their way to the morgue! (This is extremely embarassing to the medical profession, not to mention its effects on the victim's family and friends.) For this rea-son a hypothermia victim should never be considered dead "until warm and dead."

Other organ systems such as the kidneys and liver are also affected; this can lead to a decreased ability to metabolize medica-tions and other substances as well as to increased urination and hence a tendency toward dehydration.

Prevention: The key to hypothermia is prevention. I'll say it again: The key to hypothermia is prevention. Got it? Good. Many mountain climbers and explorers have suffered far colder tempera-tures and fiercer conditions than the northeastern backcountry without a problem, and so can you. In order to maintain a steady production of heat it's important to be in top physical condition, eat and drink properly and move steadily, neither going so fast as to sweat profusely nor standing around for long periods. Clothing and other gear must be kept well organized and accessible to mini-mize long stops. To cut down on conduction keep a good layer of insulation between you and the ground by using adequate foot-wear while walking and a thick enough sleeping pad at night. You may even want to bring along a small square of foam pad to use as a seat cushion when you stop to sit down. Wearing windproof clothing, using the terrain as a windbreak, and bringing a tent or bivouac sack for emergencies will help guard against heat losses from convection, while wearing a hat and keeping exposed bare flesh to a minimum protects the hiker from radiant heat losses.

Each person of course must try and be as aware as possible of his or her own body, i.e., monitor your body, and be flexible enough to make any necessary changes in pacing, clothing or even itinerary to prevent chilling. In more advanced hypothermia, however, the individual can no longer accurately assess what's going on, so it is also a good idea to keep a careful eye on one's companions, especially those with less experience. It must be pointed out, however, that experience is no guarantee of protection from hypothermia, and many very capable hikers and climbers have fallen victim to it.

Treatment: Mild to moderate hypothermia is by far the most common form encountered in winter backpacking situations and so, although the use of sophisticated medical techniques for rewarming profoundly hypothermic persons may be interesting, the major emphasis on teaching treatment of hypothermia is and should be on simple early measures to prevent a relatively minor disorder from becoming a major disaster.

While the victim is still walking and talking, further heat losses should be immediately reduced by getting that person out of any wet clothing and into dry things, with special attention to major areas of heat loss such as the head, neck and trunk. Protection from the wind should be sought, either with clothing, shelter, or a change in the route. The next thing to do is try to increase heat production by feeding the person easily digestible foods such as carbohydrates and warm (not hot), sweet liquids. Under no circumstances should alcohol be given. After changing the victim's clothes, giving some food and allowing a rest, the party if possible should resume moving. This has been called the "Feed 'em and beat 'em" approach, and in the majority of cases, it works.

The order in which these steps are undertaken depends on the circumstances. For example, if the group is only 100 yards from shelter it may be best to press on ahead and treat the problem there. On the other hand, if the hypothermia is more advanced, a distance as short as a quarter of a mile may take surprisingly long and the few short minutes required to help the victim change clothes and have something to eat may be crucial later on. Remember, the earlier the problem is spotted, the simpler the treatment will be.

If all of the above steps have been tried and the victim still can't warm up, it may be necessary to try actually adding some heat, although this is not easy in the backcountry. Giving warm liquids will add a little, but compared to the total amount of heat in one's body, the amount that can be added by drinking warm liquids is so small as to be almost insignificant. There is, in fact, a theoretical concern that hot liquids may cause cold blood from the extremities to be returned to the core too quickly.

The time-honored method of putting the hypothermia victim in a prewarmed sleeping bag along with another warm person ("buddy bagging") is possibly overrated, but when all else fails it's worth a try. Some groups carry a few of the "strike-to-activate" hot packs that can be found at most drug stores; if placed around the victim's neck, groin, and armpits, these can add a certain amount of warmth. Another way to do this, if a stove is available, is heat water for "hot water bottles." More sophisticated heaters, warming blankets and jackets are used by rescue groups, but they are generally too heavy for recreational groups to carry routinely.

The worst possible scenario of the hypothermic person who lapses into unconsciousness is, fortunately, very rare. The same general principles of minimizing heat loss and adding heat apply, but it must be kept in mind that the hypothermic heart is extremely sensitive. If jostled too much a cold heart may stop any lingering, perhaps undetectable, activity it still may have. The comatose person with hypothermia should therefore be handled *extremely gently*. Some authorities believe that even in the absence of any detectable pulse, chest compressions should not be started because there may well be enough undetectable heart activity to sustain life, and chest compressions may cause a very slow heart rhythm to degenerate into a useless quivering or "fibrillation" of the heart. The current recommendations, however, suggest checking for pulse for a full minute, and then, if none is detected, beginning full CPR. There is a well-documented case of a man in Boston who had a completely lifeless electrocardiogram tracing for two hours and eventually recovered completely. There is some evidence that mouth-to-mouth breathing alone in such cases may be beneficial. Several good references on the treatment of profound hypothermia may be found in the back of this book. Let's hope we never really need them. If we're prepared and act wisely, as this next fellow did, we won't.

On his way out of Zealand Falls Hut in New Hampshire a lone cross-country skier broke through the ice while crossing the outlet of a beaver pond and sank in the water up to his chest. The temperature was in the single numbers and a strong wind blew out of the north. He reached down into the icy water to take off his skis and managed to drag himself back onto the ice. Once on shore he rapidly stripped off his wet clothing and replaced it with dry, gobbled a few handfuls of gorp and took a few swigs of hot tea from his thermos, scraped the ice from his skis, and headed on down the trail without incident.

Frostbite: Literally, frostbite is the freezing of bodily tissues. The actual damage it causes seems to come from the formation of tiny ice crystals in the capillaries that "draw" water out of the cells and dehydrate them, and the formation of microscopic blood clots, again in the capillaries, which block off the circulation to the areas affected. The parts of the body at greatest risk for this type of injury are exposed areas of flesh such as the face, ears, and wrists and the most "distal" extremities (i.e., the farthest away from the heart, such as the fingers and toes), progressing, in more severe cases, to entire hands and feet.

Types of frostbite: The degree of involvement of a part of the body may range from very superficial to very deep, and for practical purposes most experts divide it roughly into *frost nip, superficial frostbite, and deep frostbite.* Frostnip is a freezing of only the outermost layers of skin, usually on the cheeks or ears. It appears as a gray or whitish patch which, if recognized promptly (by one's companions, as the hiker himself will usually be unaware of it), can usually be thawed with the palm of a hand. Ordinarily when one pinches an area of skin and lets go, the blanching that occurs will disappear in one to three seconds. If the skin is pinched and the whitish color persists much longer than that, some degree of capillary injury should be suspected.

Superficial frostbite extends to deeper layers of skin. It appears as a whitish/yellowish patch that feels stiff and "waxy" to the touch, but beneath which the springiness of yet unfrozen tissues can still be felt. Thawing is painful, and the skin usually turns a purplish color and may blister. Healing is generally complete although people with more serious cases may be left with some long-term sensitivity in the area affected.

Deep frostbite freezes not only the skin but layers beneath it, including, at times, muscle and bone. The area is totally numb and feels hard, like a block of wood. Blistering is variable, and these cases require optimal care to minimize infection and tissue loss.

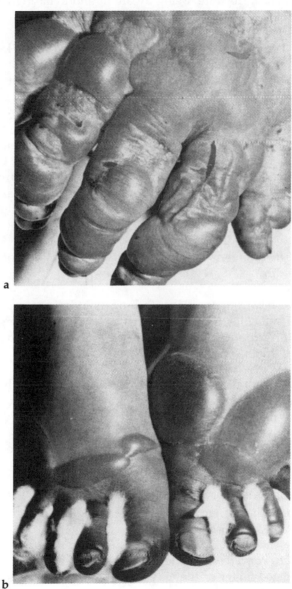

Serious case of deep frostbite. (a) No permanent loss of tissue. (b) Serious case of deep frostbite, thawed with the old ice-and-snow method. All toes were eventually lost. (Both photos were taken seven days after injury.)

Listed below are some of the major factors that can lead to the development of frostbite. Being aware of and avoiding them is the winter backpacker's best protection.

Cold temperatures, obviously; but with the proper knowledge and equipment one should be able to venture out safely in almost any northeastern winter weather. If too many of the other risk factors are present, on the other hand, one can get frostbite in very mild conditions.

Moisture from perspiration and precipitation robs heat from the body many times faster than air. Stove fuels, because of their rapid evaporation, are especially bad and can cause instant frostbite, as can freezing cold metal. Even metal earrings can increase the risk of frostbite to one's earlobes if uncovered in conditions of extreme cold and wind.

Wind further reduces heat losses (especially in combination with moisture).

Constriction from overtight clothing, boot laces, crampon straps, even the muscular tightness that comes from prolonged steep climbing or gripping of ice axes or ski poles can seriously reduce blood flow to an extremity.

Dehydration takes its toll by causing the blood to thicken and move through the capillaries more sluggishly, thus increasing its chances of freezing.

At *high altitudes* the decreased amounts of oxygen reaching the tissues make them much more susceptible to damage.

Medications and other substances that decrease circulation or production of heat—narcotics, nicotine, tranquilizers, and alcohol—are risky and should be avoided.

Previous frostbite can affect nerves and circulation so that a once-damaged finger or toe may always have an increased susceptibility to recurrences.

Here's a little mnemonic to help remember how to prevent frostbite. It goes: "Wear WILD (Windproof, Insulating, Loose and Dry) clothing and watch out for the DAMP (Dehydration, Altitude, Medications, and Previous injuries)."

Meanwhile I had gone into R.'s tent. He was appalled at the sight of my hands and, as rather incoherently I told him what we had done, he took a piece of rope and began flicking my fingers. Then he took off my boots with great difficulty for my feet were swollen, and beat my feet and rubbed me.... —MAURICE HERZOG, *Annapurna*

Treatment of frostbite: By the time Herzog's train reached Gorakhpur a small pile of amputated fingers and toes had to be swept out of the door. Knowing what we now know about the formation of ice crystals and clots in the blood vessels, it seems very obvious that such violent and vigorous methods as rope-whipping, slapping, squeezing or massaging the tissues with snow only increase the damage.

Since about 1956 (Herzog's ascent of Annapurna was in 1950) the preferred method for thawing a frostbitten part has been gentle, rapid rewarming in clean water (potable tap water is fine—don't delay treatment waiting for sterile water) between 104 and 108°F (never above 115°F). This feels warm but not hot to the touch, and it should always be tested with a thermometer prior to use or, lacking a thermometer, by immersion of an unfrozen elbow. Dry or radiant heat sources such as fires, heaters and blow-dryers must be avoided as they can easily burn an unfeeling, frostbitten area.

Often a finger or toe will have thawed out on its own by the time it's discovered, but if it hasn't, a decision must be made whether to thaw it out in the field or to wait until definitive medical help can be reached. Experience has shown that injury from refreezing a tissue seriously compounds the original injury, and it is also clear that stumping along on a frostbitten foot is relatively painless, whereas walking along on a just-rewarmed foot is next to impossible. In such situations the party must ask, "If we thaw it out and the victim can't climb or walk to safety, how difficult will it be to effect a rescue?" For example, two Himalayan climbers huddled in a tiny tent at 24,000 feet with frozen toes would probably be better off to descend first before trying to thaw out, while a winter hiker with frozen toes three miles in on a logging road may be able to make camp, thaw out his toes, and be evacuated easily by sled or snowmobile.

To prevent infection all affected areas must be kept as clean as possible, ideally covered with a sterile dressing. Blisters, which contain sterile fluid, should be protected from breaking, although under some circumstances they may be later drained by a doctor. Certain anti-inflammatory medications such as aspirin and ibuprofen have been shown to decrease the tissue damage as well, as has the local application of aloe vera to the blisters. Medications for pain are useful during the rewarming stage, which can be extremely uncomfortable. If using pain pills, give them as early as possible, as most oral pain medications take at least half an hour to work. Antibiotics are controversial unless infection has already set in, and medicines to increase the circulation have not yet proven to be of much help, although there is still active research in this area.

Other Selected Winter Medical Problems

Other, less common forms of cold injury include *trench foot* and *chilblains*. Trench foot, also known as immersion foot, looks very much like frostbite, but rather than actual tissue freezing, prolonged exposure to wet, cold conditions between about 32–50°F causes blood vessels in the feet to go into spasms, robbing the tissues of oxygen and injuring the capillaries. The risk is increased by immobility and, as the name implies, it is primarily a problem of soldiers who are forced to spend long periods standing around in cold, wet trenches. Perhaps the equivalent in winter campers would be called "bivouac foot."

Chilblains show up as reddened, roughened skin that is slightly swollen and itches. It most commonly occurs in the same areas as frostbite and is due to repeated exposures to cold, wet and wind. It is fairly common in cold weather horseback riders and occasionally runners or cyclists who get it on their thighs, which catch a good deal of the wind. The treatment is better protective clothing and an application of a soothing, moisturizing lotion.

Splinting and bandaging in the wintertime must be carefully done to avoid cutting off the circulation to an extremity. If possible, bandages should not completely encircle an injured limb. Ankle injuries can be effectively taped using a "basket weave" pattern which spares the important dorsalis pedis artery where it courses across the top of the foot.

Snowblindness is literally a sunburn of the eyes, specifically the cornea and conjunctiva (outermost layers, thank goodness). As with a sunburn of any part of the body, the onset of pain is often delayed as much as several hours following the initial exposure, during which time one may only be aware of a sensation of brightness. Typically the victim's eyes become bloodshot, irritated and painful, in some cases exquisitely so. The eyes water profusely, the lids become swollen, and any further exposure to bright light is unbearable.

The ultraviolet light rays are the major offenders in snowblindness, with long, sunny days on the snow at high altitudes (such as a day of spring skiing above treeline) being the most dangerous conditions. Whenever winter hikers or skiers venture onto such territory where they could potentially receive significant exposure to the sun, they should have one, and ideally two, adequate pairs of sunglasses or goggles with high-quality lenses and side shields to ward off rays reflected from the snow. In an emergency a pair of makeshift goggles can be made by cutting two tiny slits in a piece of cardboard, nylon cloth, or any other material that's available.

It may take as long as two or three days for the eyes to heal after a bad case of snowblindness, during which time eye patches, dark glasses, cool wet compresses and pain-killers may be used for comfort. If possible, a doctor should be consulted to examine the eyes more carefully and prescribe further treatments as necessary, although this injury usually heals well without long-term problems, so don't panic. But believe me, if it happens to you once, you'll never let it happen again.

AVALANCHES

In the winter of 1982 a rescuer named Albert Dow was searching
for two lost climbers on Mount Washington in New Hampshire.
The weather had been cold for several days, with high winds that
were dumping a lot of snow on the leeward slopes. He and his
partner were descending the Lion Head trail, one of the safest

Narrow gullies like these are prime spots for avalanches to form.

routes from treeline to the floor of the valley (although there had been a major slide near there in 1969). As they neared the bottom of the trail well below treeline an avalanche, triggered from above, swept down through the woods and engulfed them. Albert was killed. This tragic event reminded us all of a number of sobering points: fatal avalanches can occur in the northeastern mountains; they may not be triggered by the victims themselves; and trees are no guarantee of safety. It is true that such events are more common in larger mountains, but northeastern hikers should not be lulled into a false sense of security. Sizeable avalanches are often recorded in the gullies and ravines of New Hampshire's Franconia and Presidential ranges, on the great Adirondack slides like Gothics, Giant and Colden, and on numerous other lesser slopes and chutes throughout the Northeast.

Causitive Factors: In general most avalanches occur on slopes at angles of 25-45° (i.e., not always the steepest) and in areas with a past history of avalanching, but these are only statistics. Avalanches can and do occur on more innocuous-looking slopes, and the winter mountaineer should always be wary.

Other factors that favor the development of avalanche conditions include:
1. Snowfalls greater than 10–12" total.
2. Rates of snowfall greater than one inch per hour.
3. High winds.
4. Rain or major thaws.
5. Prolonged periods below freezing (due to the formation of depth hoar).

The first 24 hours after any avalanche-provoking change in the weather are the most critical, and the danger declines from there. Narrow gullies are hazardous because they tend to fill up with snow and also because they act as funnels to gather any slides coming down from above. Ridges, on the other hand, tend to be safer, and open slopes fall (pardon the pun!) somewhere between.

Types of Avalanches: Avalanches are categorized as either wet or dry and of loose snow or slabs. Wet avalanches occur during thaw periods, are very heavy and move relatively slowly, whereas dry snow or "powder" avalanches move very fast, at times riding on a cushion of air like a hydroplane. Loose snow avalanches begin as a single point and fan outwards as they go, while slab avalanches break off cleanly at what's known as the "fracture line," which may be anywhere from inches in height to many feet. As the large slab of snow slides it breaks up into many smaller slabs (which may still be larger than automobiles, even American ones) which tumble and bounce so forcefully they can crush buildings and snap off large trees like matchsticks. One shudders to think what they can do to a winter climber. Remember, "shell" clothing isn't armor.

Avalanche avoidance: Avoiding avalanches demands understanding of both the snow conditions and the terrain that produce them. Before venturing into a potential avalanche area one should consult local experts such as rangers, ski patrol and mountaineering clubs, and heed their advice. They live and work in the area and have the advantage of knowing the past history of given slopes and the pattern of snow buildup throughout the season. As shown on Table 6 (p. 69), certain snow types and terrain constitute relatively low risks for avalanches, while others are inherently unstable. However, these are only guidelines—practically any given slope can slide, and even an expert can give only an educated guess.

Most climbers will encounter eventually some questionable slopes, at which point they can: go home, detour around the trouble spot, cross their fingers and plunge on ahead, or try to obtain some more information about the snowpack before making a decision.

A quick and simple way of getting a rough idea of the snow's consistency is to sink an avalanche probe or similar device into the snowpack, pushing evenly and feeling the resistance of the different layers. If you don't have a probe use an upside-down ski pole, a ski tail, or an ice axe. Smooth, gradually increasing resistance is good, whereas sudden air pockets, soft layers on top of extremely hard ones, or pure unconsolidated snow indicate instability.

A more accurate but time-consuming way of testing the snow is to dig what's known as a test pit, digging straight down into the snowpack to expose a cross-section of the different layers. You can then determine relative consistencies by poking into the layers with a finger or credit card, or by seeing how much force it takes to pry off chunks with the blade of a shovel.

Venturing out onto a dubious slope is rarely necessary in the northeastern U.S., but if you should happen to end up in that situation, here are some tips to improve the odds:

1. If possible, head either directly up or directly down any suspicious slopes—don't traverse them. Snowshoe and ski tracks can act like a giant dotted line to shear off a slab.
2. Send only one person into the danger zone at a time. The others should be safely out of the way in a spot where they can see the full runout of the slope, so that in the event of a slide they can know where to start searching.
3. Each person should wear plenty of warm clothing, and pack straps and other gear should be loosened so as to be readily jettisoned if need be.
4. In high risk areas each party member should be equipped with an avalanche beacon. In the Northeast few people actually use these devices because of the relative scarcity of avalanche slopes, so their use will not be described in this book. They are covered very well in several of the avalanche books in the bibliography.

Surviving an Avalanche: In case of the worst—should you or a member of your party be caught in an avalanche—the following steps should be taken:

Table 6
Relative Risk Factors for Avalanches

	LOWER RISK	HIGHER RISK
SNOW	• corn • consolidated "old" snow • age-hardened snow (*sastrugi*)	• powder or windslab • more than 1"/hour • more than 10–12" total • rain, major thaws
TERRAIN	• ridges • densely wooded areas • windward slopes	• gullies, old avalanche paths • open slopes 25–45° • S to E-facing slopes

For The Victim

1. Jettison any encumbering equipment, including pack and skis.
2. Fight to stay on top of the snow, feet downhill in a sitting position if possible. Sometimes this is referred to as "swimming." Thrash, flounder, flail—whatever it takes.
3. Try to work yourself toward the side. Many early slides are fairly narrow and one can sometimes escape from them.
4. If you're still in the slide as it comes to a stop, sweep out a space with your arms in front of your face and take as big a breath as you can to expand your chest, for when the snow stops it will "set up" like concrete. Try to poke a hand or a foot to the surface, but if your initial efforts to break free are unsuccessful you must stop struggling and conserve oxygen. If you hear voices or footsteps, cry out, but otherwise save your energy—sound only travels a matter of inches in consolidated snow.

For The Witness(es):

1. Identify rapidly and accurately (a) the point where the victim was struck by the slide, and (b) the point where he disappeared from the surface.
2. If there is no further obvious danger, proceed immediately to points (a) and (b) and mark them. Seconds may be critical.
3. The victim should then be roughly on a line described by (a) and (b), a distance below point (b)—how far being determined by the size and shape of the slide.

In searching for a buried victim, speed is of the utmost importance. Despite the occasional account of a person surviving hours to days after being buried under the snow, statistically one's chances of survival fall off dramatically after the first 30 minutes to 50% or below. Unless extra help is only minutes away, all unburied survivors must begin an *immediate* search which is continued until everyone is found, or for at least 30 to 60 minutes, before anyone is sent for assistance.

Based on the estimated location of the victim, the area is first covered with a *quick search*, a hurried walk over the area looking carefully for clues such as bits of equipment or clothing, rocks, or tree stumps against which the victim may possibly have been pinned. When victims are uncovered alive, it is usually due to the quick search. Any clues must be carefully marked.

The next step is a *quick probe* of the most likely areas, as determined by the quick search. To probe, the rescuers line up elbow to elbow and advance in unison, plunging their probes as deeply as possible, withdrawing, then advancing another step and repeating the process. The feel of a body is altogether different from that of a tree or a rock.

If the quick probe fails, the last resort is a *systematic probe*, covering a larger area more slowly and methodically. By this time one will most likely be searching for bodies, although it is important to not give up hope.

Recovery of a buried victim, as with any medical emergency, must begin with protection of the victim's airway and cervical spine. Neck injuries are common in avalanche victims, and their mouths and tracheas (windpipes) are frequently plugged with snow, so all winter mountaineers should know how to maintain a person's head and neck in proper alignment as well as be able to clear an airway. Once these tasks are completed one can then turn to the restoration of breathing and circulation if needed, and attend to the treatment of hypothermia, frostbite, and any other injuries incurred.

Food and Drink

"And when you crush an apple with your teeth, say to it
in your heart,
Your seeds shall live in my body,
And the buds of your tomorrow shall blossom in my heart,
And your fragrance shall be my breath,
And together we shall rejoice through all the seasons."
—KAHLIL GIBRAN, *The Prophet*

BASIC REQUIREMENTS

Any way you look at it, winter hiking and skiing burn a lot of energy. Just sitting on a couch takes about 1600 calories per day for a 150-pound person. Adding in skiing or snowshoeing can up one's energy consumption by 300 to 1000 calories per hour, or more, depending on rate of travel, elevation change and snow conditions. Therefore in a full day of winter backpacking a person may use up 3000-5000-plus calories of food energy. The National Outdoor Leadership School (NOLS) recommends about 5000 calories per day for winter hiking; the U.S. Army, about 4500. Numbers aside, I think I'd rather eat at NOLS....

Every bit as important as the food we consume, and maybe even more so, is the water. There is a certain amount of water in a regular, balanced diet, perhaps up to a quart or so per day, but winter backpacking diets are notoriously dry. Add to that loss of fluids from perspiration and breathing in cold, dry winter air, and our need to consume liquids in winter becomes considerable. The problem is further compounded by the fact that cold tends to depress the body's natural thirst mechanism. As a rough guideline winter hikers should try to drink at least two quarts of water per day. Under some conditions five quarts or more per day is not unreasonable. As we become dehydrated our kidneys respond by excreting smaller volumes of a darker, more concentrated urine. If you notice your once light yellow snow turning to a dark amber color, DRINK UP! It's often said, "Keep it as clear as gin."

When to eat and drink is a controversial topic. Many people advocate sipping and snacking all day long, while others insist on sticking to "three square meals" per day. Both sides can espouse long, physiological arguments why their way works best, and there will probably always be a difference of opinion. When it's very cold most people find stopping for a leisurely lunch cools them off too much, and so adopt a "snacking mode" out of necessity. Food for snacks can be readily stored in a pocket, making it possible to eat without needing to rummage around in one's backpack. I've found it convenient to wear a very small waist pack in the front to carry snacks and other often-needed small items such as a map, sunglasses, etc. Other hikers like to use pockets attached to their pack's shoulder straps. However you choose to take sustenance, it is important to plan ahead and replenish your energy stores before that two-mile long, exposed summit ridge or that gruelling uphill scramble. If you find yourself slowing down and feeling unmotivated for no apparent reason, so-called "mountain lassitude," it may very well be due to dehydration or the need for a few additional calories.

WHAT TO BRING

A great deal of suitable winter hiking food can be found in your own kitchen cupboards or neighborhood grocery store. For short trips cereals, breads, grains, dried fruits, cheeses, dried meats, candies and crackers all make excellent fare, without having to resort to the more expensive specialty freeze-dried foods. For excursions longer than three or four days, however, the savings in weight may be worth the extra expense. There are quite a few dried, prepacked meals in the grocery stores these days, such as Alfredo noodles, beef almondine, chicken with rice, to name just a few. Beware the "suggested serving sizes," though—the average winter backpacker usually needs two to four persons' worth.

Many excellent books have been written on alpine cuisine (see bibliography), but I tend to share the opinion of Harvey Manning, author of *Backpacking: One Step at a Time*, that "most backpackers worry excessively about food." Most northeastern winter campers go out for one or two nights at a time, rarely for more than a week. It stands to reason that the longer a trip is, the more important going light, counting calories and balancing proteins becomes, but for two- and three-day backpacks most people should choose things they like and are used to preparing in the backcountry. Perhaps the single most important thing about food in the wintertime is to be sure to bring enough: enough calories and enough mixes for hot drinks. Taking in too few calories is a major contributing factor in both fatigue and hypothermia. Dehydration, as previously mentioned, can not only lead to "lassitude" and fatigue, but may also increase one's chances of frostbite.

In general, most groups find they need between two and two-and-a-half pounds of food per person per day. This can add up to considerable weight for an extended outing, in which case leaving well-protected food caches along the route beforehand may be a useful option. In addition to being plentiful, the ideal winter hiking foods are, of course, tasty, varied, easy to digest, difficult to freeze, nutritious, reasonably easy to cook, and sturdy (to resist being crushed in a backpack). I once went on a two-week backpack with a fellow who brought nothing to eat but fifty-two "sesame burgers." Needless to say, in spite of his being a vegetarian, the minute we left the woods he sprinted for the nearest hamburger stand! The point is, even a favorite food can grow old, and on longer trips variety becomes very important in maintaining group morale. As far as the blend of proteins, fats and carbohydrates in a diet is concerned, most Americans eat too much protein and fat, anyway; but on a cold winter's night a little extra fat helps one stay warmer. One useful analogy is to think of the body as a wood stove burning kindling, sticks and large logs. The kindling (simple sugars such as candy bars) burns quickly and gives off a lot of heat, but then quickly goes out. Medium-sized sticks (complex carbohydrates like breads, pasta, potatoes, etc.) go on next to keep the fire going and heat up the room, and if we want to go to bed and be sure the fire burns through the night, we heap on a layer of bigger logs (fats).

Table 7 (p. 77) is a list of some suggested foods for winter hiking. It can be used to arrange individual "courses" of a winter meal—for example, a breakfast of hot oatmeal with dates, sunflower seeds and brown sugar, followed by a bagel with cream cheese and washed down with a cup of hot cocoa. Many winter hikers start the day with a hot drink in the sleeping bag along with a few handfuls of cold food as a way of simplifying cleanup and getting an early start. This allows them to get moving faster and get warmer more quickly than eating any number of bowls of hot oatmeal. As is commonly done with the dinner meal, you may wish to combine a number of ingredients—for example, a mélange of a starch, a meat and a vegetable. These so-called "glops," "onepots," or "hooshes" are easy to prepare, filling, and as tasty as the chef is creative. Sometimes, though, it's nice to stretch out a long winter evening with multiple courses. After all, one of the nice things about winter camping is that it gives you plenty of time to eat, sleep and think. Once camp has been made and you're snug, warm, and pleasantly tired, relax and enjoy the food and the company!

WINTER WATER

On day trips all the necessary water can often be brought from home, but on longer excursions one will need to refill along the way. The fastest and most efficient method of doing this is to find or cut a hole in the ice of a stream, remembering that winter is no guarantee of potable water. Do be careful not to fall in. Just as in the summertime, latrines should be located at least 150 feet from waterways, and water should never be gotten downstream of where people have been camping. Unfortunately, in spite of such measures, many once pure rivers and streams not only in the Northeast but in many parts of the country have become contami-

Table 7

Suggested Foods for Winter Backpacking

CARBOHYDRATES	FRUITS AND VEGETABLES	ANIMAL FOODS	MISCELLANEOUS
Grains	*Dried Fruits*	*Meats*	*Drinks*
• rice	• raisins	• beef jerky	• juice mixes
• cous-cous	• prunes	• dried sausage	• hot gelatin
• millet	• apricots	• pepperoni	• cocoa
• bulghur	• dates and figs		• teas
	• apple rings		• decaf. coffee*
	• banana chips		
Breads	*Vegetables*	*Poultry*	*Soups*
• hard, sliced	• carrots	• canned chicken	• bouillon cubes
• bagels and rolls	• peas	• canned turkey	• oriental noodles
• pita	• tomato flakes	• dried eggs	• packaged mixes
	• dried potatoes		
Cereals		*Fish*	*Spices*
• granolas		• tuna	• Use anything
• instant oatmeal		• sardines	you would at
• wheat types		• mackerel fillets	at home!
			Be creative!
Pastas		*Dairy*	
		• milk powder	
Crackers		• butter	
		• cheeses	
Cakes and Cookies			

*Caffeinated beverages should be used with *caution,* owing to their diuretic effect.

nated with harmful bacteria from human feces in addition to the nasty parasite known as *Giardia lamblia* (Giardia for short, or for those of us on a first-name basis with him which, believe me, you don't want to be!). Giardia lives in the intestines of a number of animals, notably beavers and humans, and when ingested by an unwary hiker it can cause a crampy, bloating form of diarrhea that may not occur for as long as a month after the trip is over but can last for weeks, cause considerable weight loss, and general ill humor in the victim. For this reason any remotely suspicious backcountry water should be purified. The most popular summertime methods for water purification include boiling, filtering, and chemical purification with iodine or chlorine. Water filters, although popular in summer, don't remove viruses such as hepatitis and invariably freeze up in winter, making them useless. The effectiveness of the chemical methods is related, in part, to the water temperature, and so purification of very cold water may be too slow or incomplete in some situations. This leaves boiling which, although time- and fuel-consuming, is very effective. Recommended boiling times by various authors range from just bringing the water to a boil to boiling it for ten minutes. The Adirondack Mountain Club recommends three minutes of boiling as a reasonable compromise. The risk of encountering such harmful organisms in backcountry water is especially great following thaws or rains which wash harmful critters into the streams from the soil in droves. Despite all these precautions, should you come down with a diarrhea that lasts more than a week, you should seek medical attention, and stress to your health care provider that you were just on a camping trip. There are a number of medicines that will cure Giardia infections, although it is important to remember that not all of these backcountry intestinal bugs are Giardia; it may also be a virus or bacterium, or even just too much dried fruit. Sorting this out may take some time and a number of specimens.

If there are no sources of running water nearby, the winter camper must melt snow, which consumes considerable amounts of time and fuel. The most efficient way to do this is to begin with a couple of inches of warm water in the bottom of the pot and then add the snow gradually to that. Never start with just snow if at all possible because the bottom layers may melt and vaporize, leaving an air space over a dry pot—a sure way to ruin it. Most people like to keep this chore down to once a day, if possible, usually in the evening. To keep the hard-earned water from freezing one can either store the water bottles in his or her sleeping bag overnight (be sure the caps are screwed on tightly!) or bury them at least a foot below the surface of the snow, allowing Nature's natural blanket to keep them warm.

During the daytime several options are available to keep water from freezing. An unbreakable thermos is effective but heavy (although it is nice to have a cup of hot tea or the like during the day, especially in case of an accident). A regular water bottle can be made into a thermos of sorts by insulating it. In milder conditions sometimes all that's needed is an old wool sock; when it gets colder a pouch of closed-cell foam, homemade or bought, will often do the trick. Another method that's been used by winter hikers for years is simply to carry a water bottle inside your shirt, sometimes on a string around your neck or in an inner pocket, allowing your own body heat to keep it from freezing. This has the advantage of making the water more accessible and reminding one to drink more often, but many people complain this makes them feel like a Saint Bernard.

COOKING

The snow from the topmost bough was the first to fall, striking and dislodging the snow on the boughs beneath. And all this snow, accumulating as it fell, smote Tom Vincent's head and shoulders and blotted out his fire. —JACK LONDON, *To Build a Fire*

If only Tom Vincent had carried a lightweight, single-burner, petroleum-fueled backpacking stove, this hero of Jack London's classic tale of hardship in the cold, frozen North might have reached Cherry Creek Divide with no more than a rosy glow to his cheeks. As many winter travelers since have discovered, building a cooking fire in winter can be tricky at best, not to mention the impact that campfires make on the environment in terms of trees and branches cut, smoke, and ashes. As has often been said, "Fires last a night; fire rings last a decade." It is true that wood is a more easily renewable resource than gasoline, and I hear this argument along with "Someone who knows what he's doing can build a low-impact woodfire," but experience has shown us time and again at popular camping areas all over the Northeast, that most people do *not* know how or care to cut only dead and downed wood, keep their fires small, and remove all traces of the fire before they leave. As someone who heats his home with wood I'm not opposed to wood heat, however, I think for winter backpacking in most parts of the U.S., small backpacking stoves are really the way to go.

Liquid and bottled gas fuel stoves make up the bulk of the market, with innumerable makes and models available. Basically each of these stoves is made up of three main components: a fuel

Types of stoves. (a) A well-worn, sturdy and dependable liquid gas stove. Note the pump handle on the end of the fuel tank. (b) A lightweight liquid-fuel stove that uses the fuel storage bottle as its fuel tank, and burns anything from moonshine to rocket fuel. (c) Bottled gas stoves are simple, quiet, and clean, but may not perform as well as others in the cold.

canister or tank (with or without a pump), an on/off adjustment valve, and a burner assembly with rack to hold the pot in place. In the canister stoves, butane or liquified petroleum gas (LPG), or a mixture of gases, comes already compressed in a cylinder, a scaled-down version of the propane tanks used in people's homes. Lighting them is simple and clean, requiring only popping on the canister, lighting a match, and opening the valve. The disadvantages are that the fuel cans are more costly than plain liquid fuels, aren't refillable and hence create a waste problem, can be hard to find in some areas, and in cold temperatures the pressure inside the cans goes down so in order to start them the fuel canister must be prewarmed—inside one's sleeping bag or shirt, for example. Still, because of their ease of operation and maintenance some winter campers prefer them. This type of stove works better at high altitudes, where the decreased barometric pressure offsets the decreased canister pressure due to the cold. Likewise cold-weather performance is better with some of the newer fuel mixes, e.g., propane/butane, but for very low temperatures I'd stick with a traditional liquid-fuel stove.

The liquid-fuel stoves, burning usually either gasoline, kerosene or alcohol, have long been the standard against which all newcomers are judged due to their relatively low cost, worldwide availability of fuels used, and their dependability in a wide range of conditions. The fuel is stored in a bottle or tank and is delivered to the burner either by a pump or prewarming, which causes it to expand. For winter use, a pump is a very desirable option, as prewarming takes considerable time and generates significant frustration in certain conditions. Additionally, the use of a pump minimizes the risk of spilling the fuel, which can cause instant frostbite upon touching bare skin due to its rapid evaporation. To start the stove running, a small amount of fuel must be burned to heat the fuel line and burner enough that it actually vaporizes the liquid. This can be done with a small amount (usually one teaspoon or so) of the fuel itself, or more safely with a dab of one of the commercially-prepared fuel pastes that are made for this purpose. Some hikers carry a small squirt bottle of a fuel such as alcohol for this, but I always find the fewer bottles of spillable fuel, the smaller the chances of error. Thus, these stoves actually burn vapors rather than the liquid fuel itself, which is why most of them sound and heat like blowtorches. During this initial "priming" step it's important to **not open the adjustment valve too quickly.** If you do, the stove will spew an aerosolized flame about three feet into the air and can easily ignite a tent or anything else in the vicinity. Many hiking clubs and schools strongly insist on doing all of their cooking outside of their tents, citing scores of frightening cases of tent fires and carbon monoxide poisonings. While these are real hazards, in some situations, e.g., above treeline in a blizzard, this is not possible, and so one is forced to cook inside at least an entryway or vestibule. In these situations keep the stove as close to the entryway as possible and a leather mitten or some other suitable potholder nearby so that a flaming hot stove can be quickly hurled into the snow if it erupts. Good ventilation is also a must. Carbon monoxide poisoning has indeed killed a number of unsuspecting campers and climbers, and may have contributed to lack of success and poor judgment in others. I once tried to heat my car with a camp stove (its own heater was broken). Maybe that's why we never got to the climb....This is not a recommended use of a stove, although for my next car I'll probably look for one with a vestibule. In a tent try to unzip as many openings as possible, and minimize the cooking time, for example by choosing dishes that only require hot water. In an igloo one must create at least one, and preferably more, ventilation holes, and poke them open periodically with a ski pole or ice axe if it's snowing.

In choosing a stove one will want to consider a number of factors:

Size and weight. Lightest is not always best, however.

Stability, both of the stove on the ground and a pot on the stove. While on one of my first extended winter camping trips I had the unfortunate experience of watching a pot full of water slide off the top of a stove and into my sleeping bag. Fortunately we were able to wring it out to make soup. Yes, it was a duck down bag, but I don't think this is where the Marx Brothers got the name for their film. They were not much for winter camping.

Ease of operation, cleaning and repairs.

Type(s) of fuel burned. There is at least one model on the market that will burn anything from moonshine to rocket fuel, a consideration for backpackers who travel to far-away lands, or when I visit my relatives in West Virginia.

Performance, including the ability to simmer, something many stoves lack. In general one should count on one-quarter to one-half cup of fuel per person per day, depending on the complexity of the meals and the amount of snow melting that needs to be done. To save on wasted heat a windscreen can be fashioned from aluminum foil or similar material and used to surround the stove and pot.

Last but not least, consider the **cost**.

In addition to a stove, one will of course need some cookware. My advice here, as in most of the rest of the book, is to keep things as simple as possible. One of the major mistakes we see over and over in novices is carrying a too-heavy pack, so leave the omelet pans and easy-bake ovens behind. A single large pot should suffice. If your cook kit has two pots, as many of them do, consider leaving one of them at home, although a second pot can be helpful for scooping snow to be melted. There are some other accessories, however, one may wish to consider. A foldable aluminum windscreen can be a lifesaver for "al fresco" cooking, and also helps improve fuel efficiency by decreasing heat losses. Likewise an attachable "heat exchanger" that wraps around the cook pot may be worthwhile, especially on longer trips where the savings in fuel offsets the additional weight. A very handy item is the stove platform, a small piece of material on which to set the stove to help keep it level and prevent it from melting down into the snow or, worse, into the tent floor. Some people use a square of old ensolite for this, but with many stoves the heat blasting downwards is too great, and so a harder, less meltable material such as a piece of 1/4 inch plywood or a sheet of thin metal (a good use for an old license plate) is better. The problem with metal is that it's sturdy, but not a very good insulator, leaving the tent floor still at some risk.

Beginning winter campers should be aware that often times things don't work as well in the winter as in summer. Stove parts freeze and tiny foil packets fight to stay closed, among other things, so it's a good idea to familiarize yourself with your stove's cold weather peculiarities before embarking on a trip. A good test is to cool the stove off in your freezer over night and then try to light it. Be careful not to light a frozen dinner instead. It also helps to perfect one's camping cookery in the warmer months—a winter trip is no time to learn how to operate your stove or to learn how to cook! As I've already said, keep winter meals relatively simple and easy to prepare, at least when starting out. Many winter campers use only one pot and learn to adjust to the occasional grains of rice in their cocoa, or cook meals that only require the addition of hot water, e.g., instant soups, certain freeze-dried foods, etc. As one of my friends pointed out, you may have to think twice before bringing a winter camper home to meet Mother. After all, who wants a son- or daughter-in-law who goes for days without bathing and drinks dishwater!

CLEANING UP

One nice thing about cooking in winter is that food scraps inside dishes and pots will quickly freeze and then can be (usually) scraped out with a spoon or a scrub pad. This can be done prior to making an evening drink which will rinse out the rest. I like to use a single large mug, starting with soup, then the main course, then a cup of cocoa that camoflages the food particles, and finally a nice cup of tea, that leaves my mug clean and ready for morning. All food scraps, wrappers, cans and other containers should of course be carefully stored and packed out.

If you can carry it in, you can carry it out!

Clothing

"Now I out walking
The world desert
And my shoe and my stocking
Do me no hurt."
                          —ROBERT FROST, "Away!"

An exhaustive discussion of all the makes and styles of winter clothing available would be exhausting, not to mention the fact it would be outdated before it was printed. What follows are some basic principles of dressing for winter that are as true for those in gunny sacks and garbage bags as for those in designer pile pants. After that comes a discussion of some of the more popular materials in use today and, finally, a brief description of the standard articles of alpine apparel in terms of what's currently available and the most desirable features to consider.

Before buying out the local camping store, remember that backcountry clothing is a multi-million dollar business. While proper clothing is certainly important, one does not always need the most expensive item in each category. One has only to glance at a few pictures of native peoples of the arctic or the early polar and alpine explorers to be impressed by what can be accomplished with "inadequate" (by today's standards) equipment. Perhaps as important as what one is wearing is how one is wearing it, and how one adapts to its usefulness and limitations. Many quite satisfactory items such as wool sweaters and ski hats may be hiding in closets and drawers, and others may be purchased cheaply from thrift shops and surplus stores or newly constructed from scratch or from kits. My first pair of winter hiking pants was a tightly-woven pair of wool trousers from the "Pink Door Thriftshop" in Boulder, Colorado, costing the grand sum of 75¢. It took some doing to talk them down from a dollar, but I threatened them. (Author's note: Don't do this.)

THE PRINCIPLES: LAYERING AND PACING

Layering

In order for insulating clothing to be maximally effective, it must remain dry. When the newer synthetic fibers came out, some hikers decided it was no longer necessary to worry about wetness; these "miracle fabrics" would do all the work. Not true! Although it is true that synthetics dry faster than wool, it is still very possible to overheat, sweat, and then get chilled in polypropylene, polyester, or pile. Believe me, I've shivered in all of them. To keep clothing dry, not only must it be protected from precipitation, it must also be guarded from perspiration (both in the form of visible sweat as well as the moisture that is being constantly released from our skin, the so-called "insensible" loss). Presently there are two different approaches to solving this problem. In the breathable approach the clothing works as a sort of one-way valve, "wicking" moisture away from the body, on through the insulation and out through the outer layers where it can evaporate. The main layers consist of:

1. A transmissive *underwear layer* that's relatively thin and conforming and easily encourages the passage of moisture away from the skin.
2. An *insulating layer*, i.e., shirts, pants, sweaters, etc., that traps a layer of "dead air space" to keep in body heat and keep out the cold.
3. A protecting or *"shell" layer* that fends off wind, water and

wear, but still allows moisture to escape from within, either by venting or by virtue of its material (e.g., Gore-Tex®).

In the vapor barrier approach, the goal is to actually trap the moisture next to the skin so that it never reaches the insulation at all, similar to the vapor barrier in a house. Here a waterproof "vapor barrier liner" is placed right next to the skin or over a thin layer of underwear (for comfort, mainly), so all the moisture released by one's skin is contained. Initially it might seem this would make the wearer clammy and cold, but actually what happens is an equilibrium is reached so that one stays only slightly damp, but warm, as if in a diver's wet suit. After the vapor barrier liner (VBL, for short) the insulating and protecting layers are basically the same as in a breathable system, except now the shell doesn't need to breathe and so can be made more waterproof. VBL's have been used with success in all types of winter clothing as well as in sleeping bags, and seem to work especially well inside socks, probably because even leather boots don't breathe very much, and most people's feet perspire. Does that sound like Mom's old trick of putting plastic bread bags inside your rubber boots? It is! Too bad Mom didn't have a good patent lawyer. It should be noted that since little or none of the perspiration escapes, neither does its odor. This can be a particular concern on extended trips and for one's tentmates, although it has never bothered me personally. On the other hand, I seem to keep losing tent partners....

Under extreme conditions the three or four layers are used simultaneously, but in many situations a winter backpacker will need only two: underwear plus shell may be plenty for warmer days where some extra protection is needed only from wind, precipitation or branches on a bushwhack; or on a calm, colder day one may be comfortable with inner layer plus insulation, leaving off the shell. Newcomers to winter sports are often astonished at how much heat an active body produces and how little clothing it takes to keep warm while moving, yet how quickly one cools upon stopping. By having multiple thin layers of clothing rather than one or two very thick ones (such as a snowmobile suit or fur coat) the winter hiker can readily adapt to the changing conditions.

Pacing: The Strippers and the Comfortably Cool

Stepping out of the car onto a windswept, icy parking lot are two breeds of winter backpackers. The "strippers" start out warm, clad in bundles of luxurious clothing. They plan to stop several minutes down the trail to strip down, filling their deflated packs with the extra layers. The "comfortably cool" start out lightly dressed so they won't need to make a strip stop. They're the ones who keep pacing around grumbling, "When are we going to get going?" Both schools of thought have their merits and it takes a certain amount of practice to know just how much clothing to wear at the start of a day. I tend to use my toes as thermometers—if they're chilly I hang on to that extra layer. I find it much easier to keep my toes warm than to warm them once they've been chilled.

By now it should be clear that the name of the game in cold weather clothing is temperature regulation. Our bodies are remarkable creations, but in order to survive we need to maintain a fairly constant internal temperature of about 98.6°F (37°C). The best way to help our physiology is by adjusting our pace and our clothing appropriately. Too hot? Try taking off your hat for a minute, or unzip your parka or pants (among friends). Suppose you've been breaking trail for an hour, sweating and straining while everyone else is starting to chill. The solution? Step to the rear and let somebody else have a go. The deeper and tougher the trailbreaking, the more often a group should switch leads. In difficult conditions it's not unusual to change as often as every five or ten minutes.

Because of the time eaten up by frequent clothing changes, winter hikers tend to try to maintain a fairly constant energy output and move at a somewhat slower and steadier pace than in the summertime. To look at a group of winter hikers plodding slowly along, chewing their gorp and sipping from bottles slung round their necks, one could possibly get the idea that winter backpackers are a rather boring lot. Fortunately we know better!

MATERIALS

As recently as fifteen years ago nearly all winter backpackers clad themselves in as much wool as Little Bo Peep's pals and wouldn't be caught dead wearing synthetics like pile. Remember when the polyester suit was a metaphor for cheapness? As with other styles, "Wait long enough and it will come back in fashion." Not too long ago I heard a winter hiker brag he "didn't have a stitch" of natural fiber on his body. Go into any outdoor supply store and you're instantly deluged with "hi-tech" names like polypropylene, Thermolactyl, Quallofil® and Hollofil®. I've even heard about a manufacturer who's marketing a new type of sleeping bag insulation called "swallowfill," for the budget-conscious hiker.... The advantages of the synthetic fibers are clear. They do absorb water less readily, dry faster, and are often lighter, cheaper and stronger than their natural counterparts. The main disadvantages are that they're made from less readily-renewable resources, although there are now some "recycled fleece" fabrics made from "post-consumer" plastics, e.g., discarded soda bottles ("Pepsi-pro?"). By all means look for these whenever possible. Since the start of the "Polypro Age" wool has declined considerably in popularity, however reports of wool's demise are, I believe, premature. A number of manufacturers continue to make fine wool clothing, and others have begun experimenting with some of the tighter weaves and less scratchy sheep. I believe they've been feeding them fabric softener. With the general movement towards recycling and the use of biodegradable materials, there is hope in some circles that wool will stage a comeback. Let's look at a few of the more popular fabrics in detail.

Table 8 (p. 90) summarizes of the pros and cons of the various materials described.

The Naturals

1. *Cotton.* AVOID IT: "Cotton kills." Though comfortable and cheap on the streets, cotton absorbs water like a sponge, takes forever to dry, and is clammy and cold when it's wet. I feel so strongly about this I've even written a little poem on the subject: "Cotton: It's comfy when dry, and cheap to buy, but to wear it in winter, is a good way to die." Blue jeans, cotton tee and sweat shirts, flannel and cotton "waffle-weave" longjohns may look all right on the Marlboro man, but they don't make it in the mountains. Leave them at home!

2. *Wool.* Despite wool's recent decline, it still repels water fairly well and is known for staying "warm when wet" (although certain critics of wool call it "wet when warm"). Buy the tightest possible weave with a "hard finish" to shed the snow and keep out the wind. Nylon reinforcing, especially in socks, makes it stronger and more durable.

3. *Silk.* A comfortable, elegant fiber used mainly for undergarments (underwear, inner socks, glove liners). It does absorb a fair amount of moisture if worn tightly, and the "spun" texture, which is fuzzy with a dull sheen, is warmer than the unspun type. Its main drawbacks are its cost and the fact that it wears out fairly quickly.

Table 8

Common Fabrics for Winter Hiking

FABRIC	PROS	CONS
Cotton	None, for winter use	Dries slowly Cold when wet
Wool	Warm when wet Renewable resource Available second-hand	Somewhat heavy Absorbs some water
Silk	Comfortable	Expensive Delicate
Leather	Sturdy Comfortable Flexible Renewable	Heavy Not very warm
Nylon	Strong Lightweight Wind-resistant Easily waterproofed	Synthetic*
Polypro	Warm Comfortable Wicks moisture Lightweight	Low melting point Retains odors Synthetic*
Pile	Warm Lightweight Repels water	Not windproof Synthetic*
Gore-Tex®	Water-resistant Breathes somewhat	Dirt hinders action Synthetic*

*Note that all of the synthetics are made from less-renewable resources than the naturals, and they are also sometimes more expensive.

4. *Leather.* Traditionally, one of the marks of a true mountaineer was a well-worn pair of leather boots, but these are essentially extinct due to the lower cost and lighter weight of synthetic (plastic) and felt-lined rubber boots. Leather is still fairly popular for backcountry ski boots, where flexibility is more of a factor.

5. *Feathers.* Down feathers from geese, ducks, and other waterfowl are warm, lightweight, and easily compressible, making them suitable for large, bulky parkas and pants. When down becomes wet, however, it loses these properties in a hurry, something to consider in such a relatively damp climate as the northeastern United States. For more information on the types and properties of down refer to the section on sleeping bags.

The Synthetics: "Polly Pro and Her Sister Ester"

1. Nylon has been around quite a few years and is an extremely tough, tight fabric with a wide variety of uses, from clothing to backpacks to tents. It comes in a wide variety of thicknesses (weights) and weaves, and can be coated or laminated with polyurethane, Gore-Tex® (see below) or other materials to enhance its wind and water resistance.

2. Polypropylene hung out for quite a long time in the form of clothesline rope until somebody hit on the idea of knitting its fibers into a fabric. When worn close to the skin, "polypro," as it is called, is not only warm but it also wicks away moisture—its main claim to fame. The major disadvantages are that it tends to retain odors (especially problematic for undershirts and socks), some brands lose their wicking properties after multiple washings, and it can't take much heat (it will melt in a dryer and so must be hung up to dry). As an odor-free alternative, several other new fabrics have emerged, including:

Thermax®: Nonabsorbent, odor-free, and expensive.

Capilene®: Made up of two layers: the inner repels the moisture and the outer attracts it.

Chlorofibre: A polyvinyl chloride compound that repels the water molecules electrostatically. Because of its low melting point it can't be machine-dried either.

3. *Pile* is a knitted material of nylon, polyester or acrylic-polyester mixes, made up of many fine loops to trap air for insulation. It was used in Europe by fishermen and hikers for years before it made its way to the New World.

4. *Gore-Tex®:* In 1975 the W. L. Gore Co. came out with a porous, laminated material that quickly revolutionized the outdoor clothing industry. The way that Gore-Tex® works, in theory, is by virtue of the size of its pores, which allow uncondensed water vapor from the hiker's body to pass out, but are too small to let water droplets in. In this way the fabrics laminated with Gore-Tex® are relatively breathable yet water-resistant. At present, for a single material, Gore-Tex® probably plays this dual role better than anything else. There are of course times of extreme weather conditions, such as on long, technical climbs, when one may opt for a more completely waterproof fabric. The main potential leak points in Gore-Tex® are through the stitch holes at the seams, which are usually "factory-sealed," although in some cases it may still be necessary to do this at home with a bottle of "seam sealer" liquid. Another way in which Gore-Tex® may fail is if it becomes too dirty. For maximum efficiency Gore-Tex® garments should be regularly washed with a mild soap, although this is less critical with some of the newer "generations" (there have been several) of the material. As Gore-Tex® garments age they will lose some of their water repellency, which can be partially restored with an application of a waterproofing spray such as Scotch-Guard®.

HEAD TO TOE

Hats. Everyone agrees that the head and neck are major sources of heat loss, with estimates running anywhere from 30-90% of the total (I'm not sure why the great variation between estimates, although I've always sensed that some people had less blood flow to their heads than others). Whatever the percentage, a good hat is essential. Most winter hikers prefer a hat that covers their ears well and often carry two or three types of hat on a trip: a balaclava for above-treeline travel, a medium-weight hat with good ear protec-

Wind protection is critical above treeline—note parka, goggles, and mask.

The well-dressed winter climber.

tion for most colder days, and a lightweight cap for warmer times or very strenuous exertions.

Headbands and earmuffs can be a very useful addition to a hat or balaclava for extra ear warmth, or used alone for cold ears when it's too warm for a totally covered head.

Scarves and neckwarmers. Many winter hikers and skiers like to keep their necks warm with a turtleneck shirt, but for those who find turtlenecks too warm or constricting or want a little extra protection, a short knit or woven scarf or neckwarmer will help keep this critical area of the body warm when it's needed. For those who do prefer turtlenecks, consider one with a zippered neck so it can be opened to ventilate.

Hoods. If our bodies are like miniature furnaces, then our clothes are like chimneys that channel the heat up and out. A hood, in effect, puts a lid on the chimney, trapping that already-warmed air next to our head and neck where it can do the most good. Most parkas and raincoats come with an uninsulated hood, which

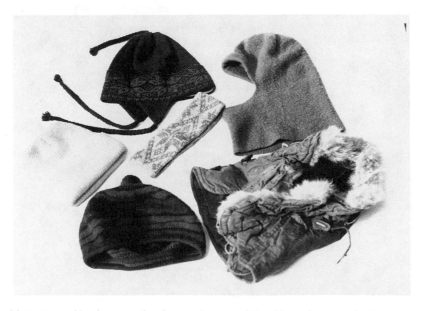

Many types of headwear can be of use to the winter hiker. Shown here are a headband, a watch cap, a Peruvian "up-down" style hat, a balaclava, an insulated hood, and a Tam-O-Shanter.

Two old reliables: the wool sweater and shirt.

Pile jackets such as this are warm, lightweight, and dry quickly.

should have adjustable drawstrings and project well in front of the wearer's face to protect it from wind and precipitation. Before buying a parka it is critical to test out the hood and be sure it fits and works properly. Insulated hoods such as the old "arctic explorer" models provide the ultimate in warmth. They have a bendable wire inside the front rim to allow it to be shaped into a tiny, sheltered tunnel, keeping out all but the stiffest of breezes.

Facemasks. Few items of clothing make such a dramatic difference in both the wearer's comfort and appearance as the facemask. One moment you're gritting your teeth while ice crystals fly into your cheeks like daggers, and the next, after slipping on a facemask, you're transported into a warm, calm, and anonymous world. I've seen a 140-pound man be confused with a 200-pound woman on account of a facemask and a few winter clothes.

Since our faces have such a good blood supply we mostly need protection from the wind. Traditionally facemasks were made from a single layer of leather, which was adequate for most winter conditions. Here, as with other types of clothing, synthetics now dominate, and most of the available masks are made from synthetics like neoprene and closed-cell foam rubber. Beware the "Spiderman" type woolen ski masks—they don't block the wind very well. Eyeglass wearers will want to take extra care to be sure

CARL E. HEILMAN II

that their mask fits snugly, especially under the eyes. This helps cut down on the perennial problem of fogging. More on that in the section on glasses and goggles.

Underwear. As previously mentioned, polypropylene or one of the polyester fabrics are the current materials of choice for long underwear due to their ability to wick moisture away from the skin. To work properly they must fit snugly so that as much moisture as possible passes through before it condenses. Prior to polypropylene most winter backpackers used woolen blends in either a solid or fishnet pattern, the fishnet allowing for somewhat better ventilation and dead airspace trapping. These are still viable alternatives and one can occasionally find polypropylene longjohns in fishnet patterns, which some people believe combines the best of both worlds. Once again, cotton long underwear, even the waffleweave "thermal" type, is unsuited to vigorous winter sports.

Sweaters and Shirts. Again, the preferred materials are wool or a synthetic like polypro or pile. A garment that opens in the front is more versatile than a pullover, although the latter may be slightly warmer. Turtleneck shirts are warmer than traditional necks, although they can be too warm, hence the previous recommendation to consider a zip-turtleneck. Two lightweight sweaters and shirts are warmer and more versatile than one very heavy one. Make sure your layers fit comfortably over each other, and be sure that the sleeves are long enough to avoid frostbite-inviting gaps at the wrists. A bulky down or synthetic parka is useful for lounging around camp, lengthy lunch stops, or emergencies, but they are rarely needed for moving about.

Shell Clothing. A shell is a thin outer layer whose function isn't so much to insulate as to protect the climber and his clothing from wind, water and wear. Thus the backpacker who sticks to the open trails may be able to get by with lighter outerwear than the bush-whacker or technical climber. Most people's shell clothing consists of a jacket and pants or jacket plus bib overalls, although some people prefer a one-piece suit. Bulky, voluminous ponchos are adequate for gentle summer rains but don't provide the wind protection necessary for most winter trips. Most shells are made of various weights of nylon, either uncoated for wind protection only or coated with polyurethane for use as raingear or laminated with Gore-Tex® for both water and wind. No matter what the material, a good shell has an adequate hood; sufficiently long sleeves with

A good shell parka, with a well-fitting hood, heavy zippers and stitching, plenty of pockets and adjustable drawstring and cuffs.

good, weathertight cuffs; sturdy zippers; double stitching; a drawstring about the waist to help keep out the wind; and plenty of pockets in which to store mittens, food and other items you want readily accessible. A good system of zippers is a must. For a parka, ventilation zippers under the armpits, so-called "pit zips" are useful, and essential for pants are, "full side zips", a set of zippers that go all the way down both legs and allow the wearer to put on or take off the pants without removing snowshoes, skis, boots, etc. In the past, when most hikers wore wool pants, it was traditional to hike in the woods wearing long underwear and pants on the lower half then, if one came to an open area (such as above treeline) to put windpants on top. Nowadays many winter hikers wear long underwear, followed by windpants (or shells), all the time. If they then encounter excessively cold conditions they must take off their windpants, add pile pants on top of their underwear, and replace the shell pants. There is something to be said for the old way here;

if only someone would manufacture either wool pants with side zippers for ventilation or synthetic pants that can be worn over underwear and still have some wind and abrasion resistance for below-treeline travel.

Mittens and Gloves. Fingers, like people, are warmer when they're huddled together, hence mittens are warmer than gloves. For fine motor skills such as working a camera, or lighting a stove, gloves allow for more dexterity. Just as multiple thin layers are more useful than single thick ones for jackets and pants, so the layering principle comes into play with handwear as well. The usual combination is one or two "inner" layers of mittens or gloves worn under a thin, water-resistant and durable shell or "overmitt." The same materials are used as for other types of shell clothing—a heavy weave of nylon, which may be laminated with Gore-Tex® and have a non-slip grip of leather, neoprene, or rough-surfaced nylon on the palm. The inner mitts or gloves are usually made of polypro or silk when maximum dexterity is needed, or wool or pile for thicker, warmer inners. Many people prefer to use three layers of handwear: a very thin polypro or silk liner, a heavy pile or wool mitten, then an overmitt. In this way they can always have a thin liner on so as to be able to take off the mittens, and still have something on their hands to do fine motor tasks. I personally find my hands seem to feel warmer without the thin liner glove, but that may be psychological (i.e., "finger separation anxiety").

When buying mitten/glove combinations it is important to be sure that each layer fits over the preceding one easily. Many a beginner has bought a pair of too-tight overmitts and discovered it too late at treeline in a howling wind. The overmitt should have a long cuff or "gauntlet" that extends several inches up the forearm, thereby covering any potential frostbite-inviting gaps at the wrists. In general it's a good idea to learn to make as many adjustments of clothing and gear as possible with one's mittens on so that in very severe conditions such tasks as replacing a slipping crampon can be done with safety and speed. In a tragic accident in New Hampshire's northern Presidential Range during the winter of 1993-94 a hiker took off his gloves in severe conditions to help his hypothermic partner into a sleeping bag and his hands grew so cold he was then unable to put his gloves back on. He struggled on for help, holding his freezing hands under his armpits, and suffered severe frostbite as a consequence. Although it is often more difficult and time-consuming to perform such tasks with gloves or mittens on, in some conditions there is no other safe choice, and it is really not as hard as many people think.

It is advisable to carry at least one extra pair of mittens per person although, in a pinch, a thick pair of socks will work reasonably well. To prevent having a loose mitten blown away by an above-treeline gust, many climbers attach their mitten shells to a long "idiot cord" which is then looped around the back of the neck. These can be difficult to manage, however, often becoming entwined in one's other clothing and backpack. A useful alternative is a loop of cord sewn inside each individual mitten that is then snugged up against the wearer's wrist with a toggle or cordlock. Some winter hikers find all of these things a bother and prefer to just stuff their mitten shells in a pocket on the rare occasions they take them off in such conditions.

The Lower Half. No matter what type of legwear you choose, from the traditional tightly woven, hard-finish wool Air Force trousers to lycra/pile/polypro overalls, pants should meet certain criteria. To begin with they should stretch or fit loosely enough to allow room for multiple layers of upperwear. Stitching should be double and reinforced at all key stress points, and areas of particularly heavy wear such as in the knees and seat may benefit from a double layer of material. The pants themselves don't necessarily have to be all that heavy, because the layering principle will be used. On colder days one can use heavier underwear, and when the wind kicks up a pair of shell pants can be added on top. Heavy wool "lumberjack" pants are really too heavy for most active uses in a layered system, and the same thing holds true of those thick, luxurious pile trousers—they're great for hanging out around camp, in bivouacs or during emergencies, but not too many winter backpackers in the Northeast actually hike or ski with them on, unless it's extremely cold.

In almost all the old photos "alpinists" can be seen wearing climbing knickers. The one advantage knickers have is a slightly increased freedom of movement at the knee, but one must weigh this against the extra cost of buying special long "knicker socks" and the nasty tendency most knickers have of pulling up at the knee and exposing bare flesh. One way to cut down on the replacement cost of knicker socks is to take an old pair that's worn out in the heels and cut off the feet, making a sort of "calf warmer" which, when combined with a regular sock, will cover the area in question. For the most part, however, with newer stretchier materials and so on, knickers seem to be going the way of the buggy whip.

Another option in pantwear that's becoming more popular are the bib-type overalls first used primarily by ice climbers and cross-country ski racers. These are very snug and warm, but they can make it more difficult to change upper layers or heed the call of Mother Nature. Different options for layering systems of underwear/pants/shells are discussed in the preceding section on shell clothing.

SAFE SOCKS

The only things worse than cold fingers are cold toes. Toes are the most susceptible parts of our bodies to serious frostbite, yet absolutely critical to our ability to move about in the backcountry. You must love your toes. For most activities at least two pairs of socks are needed: a thinner liner sock of wool, silk, or polypro-like synthetic; then one or two thick outer socks of tightly knit wool or synthetic. Between inner and outer socks many hikers use a vapor barrier liner which can help considerably, especially for people whose feet have a tendency to sweat easily. Out of the bitter personal experience of having had frostbitten toes which are now permanently sensitive to the cold (Pity, your honor, I was a young and foolish adolescent at the time!), I have come up with the following **Ten Tips for Toasty Toes:**

1. *Don't be "oversoxed."* More socks may be better, but not if it means cramming them into an already overtight boot, thereby constricting the circulation and actually making things worse.
2. *Stay loose*—gaiter ties, loose boot laces, not overtight crampon straps or snowshoe bindings. Anything that could decrease the circulation to the foot must be carefully scrutinized.
3. *Work from the ground up.* The major source of heat loss from the feet is by direct contact with the ground, i.e., conduction. Consider adding a thin inner sole of cork, foam or neoprene, as long as this can be done without making the boots too tight.

4. *Start out with warm feet.* Keep your boots inside your car en route to your destination, or in your sleeping bag in the morning. Don't throw on icy boots that have been left in a trunk or snowbank.
5. *Keep your feet dry.* Don't tromp around inside for hours with full footwear on, causing your feet to start sweating. Consider a light coating of foot powder or anti-perspirant on your feet before you start out.
6. *Keep your body warm.* If your core is too cool it will cut down the bloodflow to fingers and toes in an effort to save heat. Remember the old saying, "If your feet are cold, put on a hat!"
7. *Drink plenty of liquids* to keep your blood flowing smoothly and avoid nicotine, which makes blood vessels constrict.
8. *Try a vapor barrier.* Remember those plastic bread bags kids wore over their socks in the winter? By going directly over the foot or between the inner and outer socks, a VBL (vapor barrier liner) sock keeps the foot moisture out of the outer socks as discussed in the "Principles of Clothing" section.
9. *Take a rest stop.* Stop, you say? Yes. If you've been chugging along up the mountain and are starting to sweat but your toes are still cold, it may be that what's constricting the flow of warm blood to your feet is actually your muscles. Often all it takes is to stop for a minute, stretch your legs and shake them out a bit and voilà!, near-immediate relief. If this doesn't work try running downhill a few minutes. Often this change of muscular action will work wonders.
10. If all else fails, *stop in a sheltered spot*, put on all your warm clothes, take off your boots, and warm your toes against the belly or under the arm of a willing companion. Don't be a martyr and ignore chilly feet. It's far better to correct the problem when it comes up than to end up paying for it the rest of your life.

BOOTS

If there is a single most important piece of winter hiking equipment, it is surely a good pair of boots. To determine what types of boots to start looking at, first look at your needs. Will you be snowshoeing or skiing? Wearing crampons? Do you like to find your way to the summits, scrambling over ice-encrusted boulders, or do you prefer to stick to the valleys, camping and backpacking? Next look at your feet. Is there anything about them that would prefer a certain boot? For example, do you tend to have cold feet and therefore want a warmer model, or weak ankles and so need a stiffer boot, or fallen arches and need a sturdier sole?

Winter boots can be roughly divided into stiff vs. soft. Stiff boots are better for edging and climbing, and hold onto crampons better, whereas soft boots tend to be warmer, easier on snowshoes and, in some cases, more comfortable. Soft boots include felt-lined hunting or "pac" boots which are rubber or leather with a removeable felt liner, as well as the legendary military "mickey mouse" boots which are a layer of sealed insulation sandwiched between two layers of rubber. By sealing in the insulation the "mouse boots," as they're called, are exceptionally warm but do keep the wearer's feet slightly damp, as in any vapor barrier system. They have been used with great success in places as cold as Denali in Alaska and the South Pole. The main disadvantage of mouse boots is that crampons don't stay on them very well, and by themselves they're pretty slippery due to their flexible soles. Some hunting boots are available with stiffer lugged soles, which avoids this problem somewhat, but as the felt liners aren't sealed one must either use a vapor barrier system or dry the liners every night. It's also a good idea to carry an extra pair of liners in case of falling in water. It can be very difficult to find crampons to fit a soft pair of boots and in fact some shops are refusing to do so. Therefore, if you are considering using crampons at all, I would strongly urge you to go ahead and invest in a rigid pair of boots.

Stiff boots include single-weight hiking or mountaineering boots, and so-called double boots, which have an inner insulating boot under a rigid plastic outer shell boot. The single-weight boots by themselves are usually not warm enough for most people under northeastern conditions and their use cannot be recommended, although for some people with good circulation, adequate socks and overboots or supergaiters, they may be sufficient. The stiff double boots are the standard for difficult climbing; they edge and hold crampons well and are reasonably warm. For gentle snowshoeing or trail walking, however, many people find them too stiff, too expensive, and too heavy.

Acceptable footwear for winter hiking: (a) felt-lined shoe pac boot, military insulated "mickey mouse" boot, or double mountaineering boot (leather shown here; plastic is also acceptable). Shoes such as those shown in (b) are not recommended for winter excursions.

Once you've decided on the general type of boot you want, you will want to try some on. Wearing the sock combination you expect to be using, start out with a boot a half-size larger than your normal street shoe. Put your feet in the boots and slide them all the way forward. You should be able to slip one finger behind your heel. If you can't, try a larger size. Now slide your feet all the way back, tap your heels, say "There's no place like home," and lace up the boots. They should feel snug but your toes should be free to wiggle and there shouldn't be any painful "pressure points." If you end up in Kansas, throw this book away and find a psychiatrist, fast. Either that or watch out some witch doesn't come and steal your new boots. Try the boots walking both up and down an incline. Your toes shouldn't hit the ends nor should your heels lift more than about half an inch. Be patient. Try on as many pairs and models from different manufacturers as it takes until you get the best possible fit. Your feet will thank you, even if the sales clerk doesn't. Sometimes a wizard can help.

GAITERS, SUPERGAITERS AND OVERBOOTS

These handy items keep the snow out of boot tops and provide various degrees of extra insulation.

Regular *gaiters* are uninsulated and come either in a short (just above the top of the boot) or long (to just below the knee) length. For most backcountry uses where floundering around in deep snow is the goal, the longer gaiters are essential. Save the shorties for summer hiking or ski touring on groomed trails. Most models zip, snap or have Velcro™ openings so they can be put on after the boots. Zippers have the disadvantage of being at risk for freezing shut (although it is very difficult to find anything but), and the better gaiters are covered over by a storm flap just like shell parkas. Some gaiters are completely breathable (good for cold, dry climates), others are waterproof, and still others are laminated with Gore-Tex® or are breathable on top and waterproof on the bottom. Which type you choose will probably depend on the climate where you do most of your winter hiking, plus whichever side of the waterproof-breathable battle you fall on. The gaiter is held down to the top of the boot by a cord or strap that passes under the arch. If this is adjustable it makes for easier switching from one type boot to another, and a neoprene strap usually lasts considerably longer than a piece of parachute cord.

Supergaiters are insulated gaiters that come right down to the bootsole. They were originally developed for technical climbers, but they can be useful for improving the warmth of a marginal pair of single-weight boots. There are a number of good models on the market for backcountry ski boots as well. Most fasten to the boot with a stretchable rubber "rand" that fits snugly around the base of the boot just above the sole. Applying supergaiters is usually done with a liberal amount of thrashing and cursing, so that once they're in place, you won't want to remove them. With certain boots, however, especially the more rounded-toe models, the toes of the supergaiters may have a tendency to pop up like the hood of a '57 Chevy. This can be minimized by actually *gluing* the things in place using a stretchy rubber type cement such as Shoe Goo® or "Barge's cement."

Overboots completely envelop the boot sole and thus are warmer than supergaiters, but their use is restricted by the fact that they are too slippery to use without crampons or snowshoes.

Booties aren't for hiking, but they're wonderful in camp. These puffy, lightweight down or synthetic-filled slippers feel great after a long day of hiking, and many models are sturdy enough for the occasional 4 a.m. dash to the outhouse. Well worth considering for overnight camping in winter!

Shoe-pac and two mountaineering boots—middle with a regular long gaiter, boot on right with an insulated "supergaiter."

Shelter and Sleeping

Never so weary, never so in woe, Bedabbled with the dew, and torn with briers, I can no further crawl, no further go; My legs can keep no pace with my desires. Here I will rest me till the break of day.
—WILLIAM SHAKESPEARE, Hermia, in *A Midsummer Night's Dream*

As far as we can tell, Hermia restricted her backpacking activities to the summertime, but nonetheless, how many weary winter wanderers haven't felt exactly the same at the end of a long, tiring day? To be nestled in a sheltered spot, tucked into a nice warm sleeping bag while the winter winds howl, is one of the greatest pleasures of winter camping. Conversely, shivering away the night stiff, cramped, and praying for the dawn can make you feel like our friend Hermia, and then some.

SLEEPING BAGS

How to avoid being miserable? To begin with, a good sleeping bag and ground insulation are essential. Many winter campers purchase a heavyweight "four-season" or "expedition" sleeping bag while others supplement their "three-season" medium weight bags with liners or "overbags." The first approach usually makes for a lighter, more compact sleeping system; the second, using bags in combination, is somewhat more versatile and often cheaper overall. Manufacturers will usually suggest a "minimum comfort rating" for the bags they sell, i.e., a minimum temperature at which most sleepers will still be reasonably comfortable—a "-20°F" bag, a "-40°F" bag, and so on. (Some people say the minimum temperature rating is the temperature at which the sleeper will feel the minimum comfort!) As the manufacturer will quickly point out, these guidelines are only approximate. We all know some people are veritable furnaces in bed (or so I've heard) while others are cold under seven blankets, a down comforter and a quilt. Add to this such variables as diet, level of fatigue, physical conditioning, and acclimatization to the cold, and the temperature ratings really end up serving as only a relative index for comparing different bags from a given manufacturer.

The warmth of a sleeping bag is a function of how much dead airspace it can trap, which is due in turn to the thickness of the bag's insulation, or how much "loft" it has. Most good winter bags have from six to ten inches (or more) of loft, which generally requires from two to four pounds of insulation. This gives a total weight for a good winter bag of from about three and a half pounds minimum to six or seven pounds maximum, depending on the type of insulation that's used. Most backpacking stores can show you a table of the various weights, lofts, temperature ratings and other useful specifications for the bags they sell.

Insulating Materials

Down feathers from geese, ducks and other waterfowl have long been prized for sleeping bag fill because of their very light weight and high degree of compressibility for a given amount of loft. Left to its own devices, an ounce of good down will expand in 24 hours to about 500-550 cubic inches, which is what the maker means when he says such-and-such a bag has "550 down" in it. 550 down is very good; 600, superb. The main disadvantage of down is that it loses these wonderful properties when it gets wet, sticking together in disheartening clumps like old Cream of Wheat. *To keep your down dry:* (1) Always carry your bag in a waterproof stuff sack or plastic bags; (2) Cook outside the tent, or at least leave the bags stuffed until the cooking is done, and (3) further protect the bag from moisture by using a vapor barrier bag and waterproof overbag or bivouac sack. Some bags are made with Gore-Tex® laminated outer shells; these help somewhat but are very expensive. A vapor barrier liner (VBL) in a sleeping bag is a concept I have still not fully embraced. Many people swear by them, and I do admit I probably sleep warmer in mine, but the dampness still bothers me. There seem to be two major schools of thought on how to use a vapor barrier system to dry out wet clothing from a hard day of hiking. One group puts it between the VBL and the sleeping bag, allowing the sleeper to stay somewhat drier but partially negating the effect of the liner. The other group puts everything inside the VBL then, when it all gets good and hot and steamy, starts "pumping" the moisture out by repeatedly lifting the top of the liner and bag and letting it fall. It's almost as if the sleeping bag system becomes a giant, breathing worm: "In goes the good (dry) air, out goes the bad (wet) air."

This long-winded discussion of vapor barrier techniques fails to answer the beginner's basic question, "Should I buy a down or a synthetic bag?" In general, for cold, dry climates (e.g., the Rockies) where weight and bulk are major concerns, most people prefer down; but for extended adventures in wetter climates (e.g., the coastal ranges), one should consider a synthetic fill bag. The synthetic fills currently available are mostly different versions of polyester fibers treated with silicone to help them slip by one another more easily. Polarguard® is a solid continuous fiber, while Hollofil® and Quallofil® are short (2–3 in.) fibers with one to several hollow air tubes in them. They are all a little more bulky and heavier than down, but when wet they retain about 85% of their loft. The only possible exception to this that I know of is a new product by DuPont called "Micro-loft" whose fibers are said to simulate down clusters, and which is supposedly *warmer* than down for its weight. Time will tell. The synthetic fillings are also good for people with allergies, and generally cost about one-third to a half as much as the down.

Bag Construction

The sleeping bag filling, be it synthetic or down, must be held in place in the bag so it doesn't move around too much and create cold spots. This is accomplished by building a series of miniature partitions, called baffles, between the inner and outer wall of the bag (the liner and shell). The patterns in which these baffles are arranged are a subject of great debate in sleeping bag circles, and range from simple "box" construction to "slant walls" to "overlapping V-tubes" and so on. The main thing to avoid is the so-called "sewn-through" construction, which is literally that—at intervals rows of stitching are "sewn through" both the liner and shell, trapping the fill in little pouches. The problem with this is at each of the stitch lines the insulation is pushed out of the way, making cold spots all along the stitching. Another potential cold spot in sleeping bags is along the zipper. This is eliminated by having a long, insulated "draft tube" inside the bag which flops down over the zipper. Some good winter bags will also have an insulated tube (known as a "collar") that snugs over the user's shoulders, further helping to cut down on heat loss.

The shape of a winter bag is almost always of the "mummy" style, with a warm hood to cover the major area of heat loss, a tapered body section to minimize weight and bulk of the bag, and a somewhat roomier "boxed" toe section to help fluff out the insulation and keep the wearer's feet warm. One should consider buying a winter bag somewhat larger than a comparable bag for the summer, e.g., a "regular" sized person might buy a "large" bag, to allow room for extra clothing, water bottles, cameras, etc.

Sleeping Bag Care

A good winter sleeping bag may well turn out to be your single greatest winter camping investment; to protect your investment you must learn to care for it properly. The bag should never be stored in its stuffsack but rather should be fluffed and aired out after every trip, then placed loosely in a large nylon bag and hung in a closet or left unstuffed on a shelf. Periodically the bag will need washing to preserve its loft and improve its smell. It should either be carefully washed by hand in a large tub (e.g., bathtub) using a mild detergent for synthetics or a special down soap for feathers, or in a large, commercial front-loading washer. It should not be washed in a top-loading home washer, nor should it be dry-cleaned. To dry the bag one can use a machine, but be sure not to use much, if any, heat (never above 140°F). Adding a clean pair of tennis shoes to the dryer will help break up the clumps of down, or this can be done by hand.

GROUND INSULATION

Good ground insulation is critical, perhaps even more so than the sleeping bag itself, for it is here, through the ground, that the winter camper loses the major portion of his or her heat. Sleeping bag insulation compresses considerably under body weight, and one has only to lie on inadequate ground cover for two or three minutes before the cold can be felt at pressure points like shoulders and hip bones. To prevent this, a sleeping pad of relatively incompressible material is placed under the sleeping bag, extending at least as far down as the knees. Many campers then place their empty pack or other extra gear under their feet. Open-cell foam, the typical "foam rubber" that is found in some mattresses and sofa cushions, is sometimes used for a sleeping pad, but it is very bulky and compressible. If used in the winter it must be at least two inches thick, which means trudging to camp with a roll the size of a garbage can strapped to your pack. Much preferred is a closed-cell foam such as Ensolite® or Evasote®, the newer of which resist freezing down to minus 60°F or colder (a problem with some types that can crack at very cold temperatures). This should be at least one half of an inch thick (although up to an inch is certainly not unreasonable). The new air/foam mattresses such as Thermarest® are extremely popular, but even they usually need to be combined with a closed-cell mattress to achieve adequate protection for winter. Disadvantages of this type of mattress include the fact that some of them are so slippery you end up off them half the night, and the risk of major deflation following a "close encounter with Mr. Crampon" or any similarly sharp object.

The ideal campsite is a level spot on a south facing slope with trees for shelter, a great view, and water nearby.

CARL E. HEILMAN II

TENTS

Visit any camping or backpacking store and you'll likely find everything from A-frame pup tents that Teddy Roosevelt could have slept in to geodesic extravaganza that would leave Buckminster Fuller scratching his head. The dome shapes have grown tremendously in popularity over the past decade or so because of their roominess and tightly stretched walls, which shed wind and precipitation quite well. The shapes that can stand up by themselves without being staked to the ground, i.e., free standing, are particularly useful in winter, when it may be difficult to get a stake to hold in unconsolidated powder. Whatever shape of tent you choose, it should be easy to set up, with a minimum of parts to be dropped in the snow or delicate adjustments to make. It must provide space for all your winter equipment and have adequate ventilation for those times when you're forced to cook inside. Several

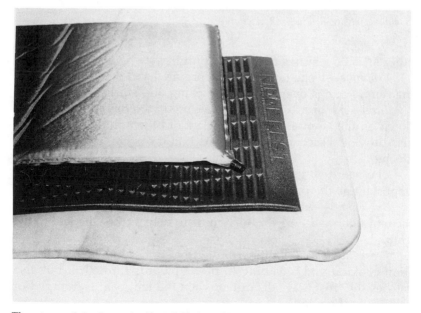

Three types of sleeping pads: (from left) A combination foam-air mattress, a ridged foam pad, and a traditional closed-cell foam mattress.

An alpine tent site high in the Rockies.

other specific features that are helpful in a "winter" tent include:

Vestibule—a sheltered extra space at the end of a tent where the rainfly hangs over, good for cooking and storing gear.

Tunnel entrances—which can be closed by a drawstring and cut down on the amount of snow tracked or blown into the tent; they also provide a second, emergency exit in the event of a fire or avalanche.

The next two items are difficult to find nowadays, and not as important as the preceding two:

Snow flaps—strips of nylon which are sewn to outside edges of the tent floor and buried under snow to help anchor the tent to the ground.

Frost liner—a fabric inner lining that not only allows moisture from cooking and breathing to pass upwards through it but also catches the frost that falls down when the tent wall is bumped or shaken by the wind.

ALTERNATIVES TO TENTS

Bivouac sacks (from the French verb "bivouaquer," meaning, I believe, "to sleep miserably"). To avoid the full weight of a tent or to sleep on tiny ledges, alpine mountaineers will often carry a "bivvy bag," a simple uninsulated sack of nylon which goes over their sleeping bag and protects them from the elements. Some of the deluxe models come with a miniature frame or hoop over the head section to form a sort of one-person tent. Although more commonly seen on difficult alpine climbs, a bivouac sack is a reasonable alternative for the go-light winter camper, and it can easily be stuffed into a hiker's daypack for shelter in case of an emergency. They are also quite useful for sleeping in snow shelters, to keep the sleeping bag from contacting the snow on the floor and the walls.

Tarpaulins and lean-tos both tend to be drafty and snow-filled in the winter, although some lean-tos are sheltered enough to make them usable or can be shoveled out and a tarp tied across the front for protection.

CARL E. HEILMAN II

Lean-tos can make good winter campsites, but may be snow-filled and draftier than tents.

Naturally-occurring shelters such as caves, overhanging rocks and the bases of large spruce trees can be fun and interesting spots to camp but can be wet or hard to find when needed, so it's best to have a tent along in case.

Snow shelters tend to conjure up images of fur-lined arctic igloos or climbers' snow caves perched high on rugged, windswept mountains. Although they can be very tight and cozy once constructed, building a good snow shelter takes considerable time, energy, know-how and the proper snow conditions. The basic types of snow houses include the igloo, which is laid up in blocks, the snow cave, which is dug from a snowslope or a piled-up mound of snow (sometimes known as a "mound house"), and the trench, which is dug into the snow but then roofed with a tarp, tent fly or other available materials.

The first igloo I ever tried to build went up and up and round and round without ever coming together. When it got about ten feet high and local farmers started asking me if they could store their hay in it, I quit and knocked it down out of embarassment. If you can learn to build a usable igloo, then making a snow cave will be easy.

For an igloo good snow is invaluable. Firm, wind-hardened snow like Styrofoam™ is ideal, and may often be found above treeline or on the surface of a lake. If you can't find any snow hard enough to cut into blocks, however, you can sometimes make it yourself by tramping out an area of powder snow then going away for an hour or so to let it "set up." You don't have to pack it down very hard; the mere disturbance of the structure of snow sets off a reaction that causes it to bond to itself. This is a good time to establish a water source, pack a trail to the latrine, build a cooking area, etc. A snowsaw to cut the blocks and a shovel to lift them free are both nearly indispensable. There are specially-made snowsaws but a long pruning saw from the local hardware store often works just as well. A fairly flat shovel is better for cutting and carrying the blocks than a sharply scooped one. Mark out an eight to ten-foot diameter circle in the snow and begin cutting your blocks from inside the circle, so that eventually the igloo will extend about as far below the snow surface as it does above it. While one person is working inside the igloo, others can start cutting blocks some distance away in the "quarry." This hole in the ground can later serve as the latrine or cooking area (not both!). In exposed areas a windbreak for the latrine is *indispensable*. Cut the blocks as large as you can comfortably handle and make the edges square (the beveling will be done as the blocks are lifted into position). The first several blocks will need to be carved to form a sort of ramp so that the subsequent blocks ascend in a spiral rather than making a series of concentric rings. As you set each block into place, you will use the snowsaw to whittle the bevel, which will be about 15° per block. I'd go through the math for computing the bevel, but who can "guesstimate" a 15° angle very well anyway? This is the art of igloo building and, like any fine skill, it takes practice to master. While one or two people are placing and shaping the blocks, any other free hands can throw shovelfuls of snow against the side of the completed work, to chink in the cracks. The entrance to the igloo should slope gently upwards to trap the warmer air inside, and it should be set perpendicular to the direction of the wind so that snow will neither blow into it nor drift over it. Keep the entrance hole as small as possible.

Snow caves and mound houses, easier to make in marginal snow conditions, are more practical for northeastern winter campers. For a snow cave one must either find a spot where the snow is at least six to eight feet deep and well packed by the wind, or pile up a mound of snow the same height, using shovels, snowshoes or whatever else is available and then let it harden, as mentioned for igloos. A good trick to cut down on shoveling is to first make a pile of all available packs and pile the snow on top of them. In that way less snow is needed to build up the house, and when the packs are hauled out through the entrance tunnel a good part of the excavating will already be done. To start the excavation, the first digger strips down to long underwear and puts on a waterproof shell in order to stay as dry as possible from both snow and perspiration. Shovels, ice axes, cooking pots and even one's hands can be used for digging. A second person can help by moving the snow that's been dug out of the way. Sometimes a small sled can be slid into the cave and filled by the digger, who then gives the command to the second to haul it away. Any others can go looking for one to two-foot long sticks to push into the snow from the outside so that the digger will have a mark to know when to stop. As with an igloo, the sleeping area should be higher than the entryway to keep the warmer air in. This can be accomplished

Using a pruning saw to cut snow blocks.

Cut as large of a block as you can possibly carry.

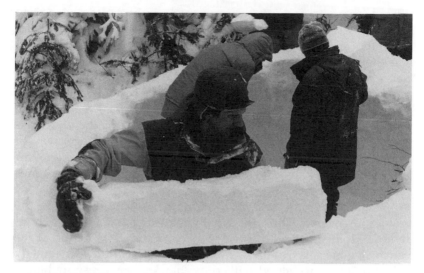

Layering the blocks.

*Home sweet home—
a cozy igloo in northern
New Hampshire.*

either by sloping the entryway upwards or by building a raised sleeping platform, which can also double as a bench.

The higher the ceiling the cooler the cave will be, but with time the roof of a snow cave will settle. If it is to be used for more than a night or two it's wise to make the ceiling a little higher to allow for several inches or more of settling per day. At first the snow will "breathe" a little, but as the cave is used a coating of ice may build up on the inside, making it airtight. It is therefore necessary to build in some ventilation. The most common way of doing this is to use an ice axe or ski pole basket to make an air hole, which may need to be cleared periodically if it becomes plugged with snow.

Snow trenches are simply long, narrow channels dug in the snow, and covered. They are usually made separately for each individual, sometimes with short connecting tunnels. The top of the trench is generally covered, or "roofed" with a tarp or tent fly staked down or weighted with snow blocks, or with snow blocks themselves. The beauty of snow trenches lies in their simplicity and ease of construction. In many snow and harsh weather conditions they are much more practical than igloos that require lengthy block-fitting efforts, or snow caves that require considerable snow depth. Their ease of construction makes them especially suited for emergency bivouacs.

MAKING CAMP

Even while planning a trip in the warmth of your living room, it's important to look over the map and start planning your campsites. The ideal campsite is level, sheltered from the wind, near a water source and, for most of us, has a nice view. One must also watch out for hazards such as potential avalanche slopes and large, hanging dead branches or treetops, a.k.a. "widowmakers." Valley sites are popular due to the availability of water, but the disadvantage is that they tend to be colder due to draining cold air from the slopes above and the fact that the morning sun is slow to reach them. A site partway up a south to east-facing slope, sheltered from the wind, with water and views, is ideal, although often one will be forced to settle for less.

Once on the trail, one should start looking for a site by mid-afternoon because of the shortness of winter days.

When the site has been chosen, the first thing to do prior to taking off snowshoes or skis is to pack out an area large enough to accommodate tent and guylines and still leave some space for walking around. The group can then delegate tasks to different individuals, such as establishing a latrine, collecting water, and building a cooking platform. During this time hikers should change into dry clothing or add extra layers before they cool off, and begin to unpack their gear for the night. The latrine area should be far enough from the campsite for aesthetics, but not so far as to prevent people from using it in the middle of the night. You will want to pack the trail to the latrine firmly enough to travel it without snowshoes or skis. It must, of course, be well away from any trails or water sources (usually 150–200 feet minimum). A cooking platform, or "kitchen" area is generally a raised or dug out "table" of snow with a good windbreak around the stove area. This makes it much easier to stand and work with a stove without having to lie on the ground. Another useful piece of construction is a "porch" in front of the tent or snow shelter. This can usually be made by going out about two feet in front of the door and digging a one to two foot pit into the snow. In this way one can come out of the tent and sit on the porch to put on boots, gaiters, etc. without having to go into spasms trying to do it inside.

For tents that use guylines, many manufacturers sell extra-wide "snow stakes" made of plastic or lightweight metal. Regular skewer-shaped summer stakes will almost never hold adequately in snow. In really fluffy powder even snow stakes may not hold and the camper may be called upon to exercise considerable ingenuity. If there are suitable trees in the area these are the easiest and sturdiest anchors. Lacking adequate trees, dead branches, or pieces of gear such as ice axes, snowshoes and skis can be plunged into the snow to provide anchors. Note that this shouldn't be done in a "base camp" situation with gear that will need to be used the next day. Another alternative is to make "deadmen" by tying the guylines to sticks, bags filled with snow or other similar objects and then burying those objects. If possible one should resist the temptation to pour water over these anchors. Although it will make them quite solid, it may also make them next to impossible to remove until spring.

Sleeping Warm

A major fear that many beginning winter backpackers have is that they will be cold in their sleeping bags. The following tips will help you stay warm through the night:

- Start with good ground insulation and an adequate bag.
- Keep your bag dry by not cooking inside your tent and by using waterproof stuffsacks or pack covers, vapor barrier liners and frost liners.
- Unpack and fluff out your sleeping bag at least 30 minutes before crawling in, allowing it to "loft."
- Be sure to eat enough calories at bedtime, and throw in a little extra fat to the evening meal. That will help keep your body's fire glowing all night long.
- Wear a hat or balaclava to bed.
- Wear as much clothing to bed as you need to. There is an old superstition that one should sleep in a sleeping bag as close to naked as possible, that somehow wearing clothing in a sleeping bag defeats the purpose of the bag. This is hogwash. Obviously if the clothing is dripping with water this is not a good idea, but otherwise put on that wool shirt, pile pants, or even heavy parka if you need to. It will keep you warmer, and save you that much time in the morning!
- If you do get cold, try doing some isometric exercises inside your bag.
- If you wake up cold in the wee hours of the morning, eat a snack. Many campers keep a candy bar or bag of gorp handy for this purpose.
- If your bladder is full, go out and empty it, or use a carefully marked "pee bottle" (mine has a Surgeon General's warning and skull and crossbones on it). It's impossible to warm up if you're lying all tensed up, and the exercise of going outside or struggling not to overturn the pee bottle into your sleeping bag will help your muscles produce some more heat.

BREAKING CAMP

One of the first things to do on your morning of departure is to pack up your tent before the snow, softened by your body heat, hardens and freezes the tent floor to the ground. Every bit as much as in summer camping, winter camping must be "clean" camping, and this can take a little more effort when it's blowing and twenty below. When leaving a campsite it's essential to make a careful search of the area for any objects that may have become partly buried by snow. Latrine areas should be thoroughly covered, and all other signs of your presence should be erased as much as possible. There's nothing more offensive for the winter hiker to come upon than an abandoned campsite with yellow snow, ashes and bits of garbage lying around. In other words, *leave nothing but snowshoe (or ski) prints!*

Other Equipment

THE BACKPACK

With all its extra clothing and equipment, winter demands a lot from a backpack. That isn't to say the same pack can't be used year-round, but there are certain desirable features that make a pack more suited to wintertime. All key stress points should, of course, be solidly reinforced. Buckles and straps should be simple and easy to operate wearing mittens. The pack should have a quick and secure system on the outside for lashing on skis, snowshoes, ice axes, and crampons that keeps them away from trees, legs, and partners. To increase the carrying capacity of a pack, attach extra pockets, or sew an extensible "sleeve" inside the mouth of the packbag to let it grow taller. This feature can also convert the pack into a fairly decent emergency bivouac sack. Some packs come with a compression system of zippers and straps that allows them to conform to the load, sort of like a boa constrictor. When considering zippers, in general, nylon resists freezing a little better than metal, but just about the only manufacturer that uses metal zippers on packbags uses such excellent ones that this isn't a problem. A loop of leather, nylon, or two to three millimeter parachute cord should be tied through each zipper handle as a pull to be grasped with one's mittens.

On the inside of the pack some backpackers prefer one single large compartment while others like smaller spaces and pockets. Like the number of rooms in a house, this is largely a matter of personal preference. I find a side pocket or two is helpful for storing a few oft-needed items such as food and water, map and compass, etc. Some hikers will also add a small pouch or two to the waistband or shoulder straps of their packs, or even carry a small "fanny" pack in the front for such items, which makes it possible to minimize time spent stopping, taking off a heavy pack, rummaging through it and hoisting it back up. Despite all of the possible modifications of big packs, most hikers will also want a smaller "day pack" for day trips from home or a base camp. This may also need to be slightly larger and sturdier than its summer equivalent.

The major decision for an overnight pack is whether its frame be "internal" or "external." For years the standard of excellence in backpacks was a rigid tubular metal frame with the packbag attached to it by pins and rings. These external frame packs have the advantage of placing the load higher, thus putting it more in line with the spine, meaning less muscular effort is needed to hold the weight up. Photos from the 1963 American expedition to Mount Everest show almost all of its members wearing external frame packs, but by the 1970s there had been a virtual revolution in backpack design and within just a few short years nearly everyone had bought a new "internal frame" pack. In this design a narrower frame of metal, plastic, or fiberglass is actually built into the wall of the packbag, making it ride closer to the wearer's back and easier to balance. It is also less likely to catch on branches, a skier's arms, or the wind, which can turn many external frame packs into sails. One further advantage of internal frame packs, for hikers who travel by airplane, is they travel much better through baggage conveyors than external frame packs do. I still remember vividly recovering my cherished frame pack at the baggage claim with one of the vertical tubes bent at a ninety degree angle where it jammed in the machinery. The airline was not particularly thrilled with it either.

*Winter backpacks are **heavy**.*

The disadvantages of internal frame packs are they're hotter to wear, not having a space for ventilation, and with heavier loads they're somewhat less comfortable than external frame packs. In summary, if you plan to be doing mostly snowshoe backpacking on trails, consider an external frame pack for its comfort and load-carrying qualities. If you plan on doing a lot of skiing, bushwhacking, or climbing, however, you'll probably want to go with an internal frame. Some people end up with both.

How to Pack It

Whether you carry your gear in a state-of-the-art technopack or your Uncle Sidney's forty-year-old Duluth pack, how you pack it makes all the difference. The principles of proper packing are as simple as ABC: accessibility, balance, and comfort. The higher the load "rides" the lighter it feels, but also the trickier it is to balance, so skiers and climbers may want to keep the weight a little lower than snowshoeing backpackers will. The heavier or denser items should be packed closer to the wearer's back, with the more frequently needed things on top. Hard, irregularly-shaped objects like cameras and cookstoves will need to be packed carefully to avoid breakage and to keep them from poking into your back. Packing food for multiple days is often a problem because it tends to be fairly heavy and fragile, hence one would want it near the top of the pack, yet putting it there gets in the way of other more readily needed items such as clothing. I generally put my sleeping bag (heavy for a single item, but not for the space it occupies) on the bottom, then my stove and tent, then the food, and finally my extra layers of clothing. Experiment around with this and see what works best for you. Whatever order you choose, remember that even though some packs are made out of waterproof material, for insurance it's still a good idea to pack any critical items like sleeping bags and clothing in waterproof stuffsacks, plastic bags, or under a good pack cover. That house on your back carries everything you need for survival. Organize it and take care of it carefully, and it will take care of you.

LIGHTS AND LIGHTING

Since winter days are short and traveling in heavy snow can sometimes take longer than planned, it isn't unusual to end a day hiking in the fading light or even in the dark, and at those times a source of light is most welcome. For camping, of course, a light is nearly essential.

Headlamps are far superior to hand-held flashlights, freeing your hands to unpack equipment, set up the tent, and hang on to your ski poles, among other things. The battery pack may either be attached to the headband directly or by a length of wire, which allows the batteries to be stored inside a warm place like your shirt. This will improve their performance, although the wires do have a tendency to catch on things unless passed out of the way under one's jacket or sweater.

There are a number of different lightbulbs and batteries available for flashlights and headlamps. The standard "PR-2" bulb found in most flashlights has a fairly low resistance and therefore requires more current and has a shorter service life than the "PR-4" and "PR-6" bulbs. Likewise, the standard carbon-zinc batteries can be improved upon by switching to alkaline or lithium cells. At 0°F a carbon-zinc battery produces only about a quarter of its usual voltage, whereas an alkaline cell holds on to about three quarters of its strength, and lithium loses almost nothing at all. Despite these significant advantages, lithium batteries have not yet completely dominated the winter backpacking market due to the fact that they are considerably more expensive than the other types, and many non-backpacking stores don't carry them. The rechargeable nickel-cadmium batteries, although superior from an environmental standpoint, have traditionally been felt to lack the necessary power and longevity for winter use, although there are now some improved models claimed to last 33% longer. I use them myself for shorter trips, and revert to the "alkies" for longer ones.

It pays to be miserly with your batteries whichever type you use, and if you allow your eyes to adjust gradually to the dark you'll find that you can get by without a light much longer than you would have thought. In fact, if there's any moon at all, the light reflected off the snow often makes it possible to hike all night

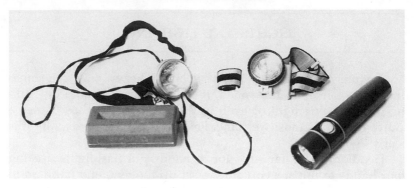

Lighting devices: (from left) headlamp with separate battery pack, headlamp with battery pack attached, hand-held flashlight.

long without a headlamp. Once someone turns on a light, however, it will take your eyes about thirty minutes to fully readjust.

For lighting inside a tent or a snowcave, a candle lantern or miniature kerosene lantern will add a surprising amount of warmth and good cheer, and can also be used as a firestarter in an emergency. This will preserve your headlamp batteries for those times when they're needed the most. Other firestarters may include waterproof matches (dip kitchen matches in melted paraffin and let it harden) and/or a tube of commercially-made firestarting ribbon or paste.

KNIVES

Just how many tools and blades should a good hiker's knife have? Nowadays you can get a knife with everything from a single blade to one that will let you make Louis XIV chairs out of spruce boughs. There are certain accessories that can come in handy for winter hiking: a hole punch, for adding holes to crampon straps or snowshoe bindings; a screwdriver (both Phillips and straight-bladed) for fixing crampons, packs, and ski bindings; a can opener; a pair of scissors for trimming moleskin and toenails; and, of course, a regular blade. I used to laugh at the two-inch saw blade on my Swiss Army knife until I happened upon an injured hiker one day and used the saw to cut down some small spruces to make a litter to carry her out.

GLASSES AND GOGGLES

If there's a chance you will be in open areas of bright sunlight for any length of time, a good pair of sunglasses or "glacier glasses" (which have shields along the sides to keep out reflected light) are essential. This is particularly true in spring, when the sun is more intense, and at high altitudes. For both glasses and sunglasses choosing plastic frames over metal will help prevent frostbite should the frame come in contact with a part of your face. Also, avoid cheap three-dollar drugstore models, as they usually don't filter out the harmful ultraviolet and infrared rays which cause snowblindness. For extended trips bring a spare pair. Contact lenses are usually no particular problem in the winter, although some types of hard lenses can pop out in a heavy wind. One should protect lens cleansing solutions from freezing by carrying them in small bottles in an inside pocket. Goggles may be useful for very high winds or when there's lots of blowing snow, although they tend to fog up more than glasses.

Speaking of fogging, the bane of bespectacled backpackers, there are a number of ways of decreasing this problem, although probably none is as good as contact lenses. To begin with, understand that fogging occurs when moisture from one's breath or skin condenses on cold lenses. Therefore it is important to decrease both moisture *and* the temperature gradient between one's face and the lenses. To decrease the moisture:

1. Don't overheat. There's nothing like dripping sweat to steam up glasses or goggles.
2. Try to breathe through your nose (rather than mouth) as much as possible, and if you must breathe through your mouth, try to exhale forcefully and downwind, to prevent the moisture-laden breath being blown back on your lenses.
3. To decrease the temperature gradient, wear goggles or glasses with side shields. Many hikers think that if they wear glasses alone, the air circulation around the lenses will prevent them

from fogging. This theory sometimes works in the woods, when it's not too cold and the hiker's not working too hard. Get above treeline in the cold and howling wind, however, and everything changes. Every breath you exhale seems to be sucked onto your icy lenses, where it instantly freezes. This happened to me on a hike up Mt. Mansfield in Vermont one winter. I was standing on the open summit, my lenses caked with ice like windshields coated with freezing rain. I took my thumbs (in my mittens), put them behind the lenses, and attempted to rub off some of the ice, not appreciating how much more the lenses had shrunk in the cold than the frames of the glasses. As I pushed on the lenses to clean them, both popped out in the snow, simultaneously. Subsequently I've found it is possible to wear both glasses and goggles together, as long as one keeps a slow and steady pace, and keeps the goggles on at all times. When you first put them on there may be an initial period of fogging due to moisture and the fact that the lenses are cold. Stay put and allow the system to equilibrate and the initial fogging should clear. After that, if you take off the goggles, the lenses will cool again, and fogging will recur. Avoid the temptation to keep removing and cleaning the goggles if at all possible; this just leads to a frustrating cycle of freezing and thawing.

REPAIR KITS

Some people like to be prepared for any possible breakdown and others carry nothing but a roll of tape for repairs. I prefer to bring several items that can be used for a variety of jobs, such as a length of nylon "parachute cord," some bendable "stovepipe wire," and white hospital tape or the wonderful gray "duct tape" (not *duck* tape), which is good for fixing everything from broken ski poles to broken bones. Sewing supplies are good for expeditions but usually aren't necessary for shorter trips, when a safety pin or two will hold things together long enough to get home. Specific tools for certain pieces of equipment usually work the best, but often a good, small adjustable wrench will suffice for crampons, ice axes, packframes and cookstoves. A large pair of pliers is infrequently needed, but a lightweight pair of needle-nosed pliers with wire cutting jaws can do everything from cut neoprene webbing to fix a broken zipper. As for screwdrivers, a shorter one with a fatter handle (e.g., the so-called "posi-drive" models) takes up less room and provides more torque than a longer, skinnier one. There are a number of tools available now such as the "Leatherman"® that combine a pair of collapsible pliers with most of the tools on a traditional Swiss Army knife, and appear to be promising. It is also advisable to bring along spare parts for any critical piece of equipment that could break down, spare crampon bails and tie rods, small screws for bindings, packs, crampons or stoves. Backcountry skiers will want to be sure they carry an emergency ski tip and an extra bail for their three-pin bindings.

A small thermometer is good for deciding on ski waxes, but it does make it harder to exaggerate about the temperature once you get home!

A rescue or emergency kit which includes such things as waterproof matches and firestarters, a whistle, space blanket, and extra food is a good idea, although many people incorporate such items into the rest of their gear. First-aid kits are discussed separately in the section on safety and first aid.

CAMERAS AND FILM

To capture some of the beauty of a winter excursion and bring home some proof to the sceptics, many winter backpackers will want to include some photo equipment along with the rest of their gear. Cold weather poses two main problems for the would-be Ansel Adams. One, it may slow down the camera and, two, it may slow down the photographer. In other words, in very cold temperatures (below about -4°F for most modern cameras) shutters may shut sluggishly, batteries may balk, levers may lodge, and fingers may fumble.

To bypass these difficulties the winter photographer may choose to leave the faithful 35mm single lens reflex (SLR) with its tripod and three interchangeable lenses behind and opt for one of the very good miniature 35mm cameras that can be kept warm in a pocket and which, with their automatic exposure meters, can shoot very good amateur quality shots with a minimum of bother. On longer trips where pack weight is a major concern or under conditions of extreme cold or difficult climbing one of these tiny cameras may be the best way to go.

Knowing all this, many winter photographers may still want to stick with their old reliables. If the temperature is above zero, most of these cameras can be stuffed in a pack or hung around one's neck and still work quite well. For extremely cold temperatures, however, one can use either a specially "winterized" camera with light-weight oil and parts machined to minimize friction, or keep the camera warm inside one's clothes. Note that if a cold camera is suddenly placed in a warm, moist environment, be it a shirt or a shelter, condensation will fog up the lens and collect on other important parts. To minimize this the camera should only be exposed to the cold for brief periods of time, but if it is allowed to chill completely it either can be gradually warmed in a room around 32°F or brought inside in a plastic bag, which causes the condensation to form on the bag and not the camera. At night the camera should be kept inside a warm sleeping bag. Cold metal parts of a camera shouldn't be handled bare-handed due to the risk of frostbite, and many winter hikers find a very thin pair of silk or polypro glove liners useful for this. It is also possible to learn to shoot most cameras with heavy mittens on, although it takes a little practice.

Film may become brittle under cold, dry conditions. It is important to handle it gently, advance and rewind it slowly, and not allow it to sit for weeks unused in the camera. Since there is usually a lot of reflected light from the snow, slower, fine-grained films (e.g., ASA 100 or less) are often the best, allowing the photographer a wide range of exposures to choose from and the sharpest images possible. Because of this brightness a skylight or ultraviolet filter should be used to protect all camera lenses, and the photographer should beware that the camera's light meter may be fooled into underexposing dark objects (like people) in the picture. For this reason it's a good idea for inexperienced photographers to "bracket" any "must have" exposures by shooting three pictures: one at the exposure suggested by the meter, another at a half-stop above, and a third an f-stop below. Some very good photographers never bracket their shots while others, including many professionals, almost always do.

Once these minor technical difficulties are overcome, many winter hikers will find that cold-weather photography not only adds another dimension to their enjoyment of the outdoors, but also provides them with some of their most striking and memorable photos.

Finding the Way

"*Something hidden. Go and find it.
Go and look behind the Ranges-
Something lost behind the Ranges
lost and waiting for you, Go!*"
—RUDYARD KIPLING

One wintry evening in a mountain lodge crowded with skiers and snowshoers I heard the following conversation:

Old Hand: So, what are you going to be doing tomorrow?
Novice: Well, we thought we'd hike over to North Twin.
Old Hand: North Twin? That's a twenty-mile round trip!
Novice: Uh huh.
Old Hand: You'll have a lot of trail breaking to do—only the first three miles are packed out.
Novice: Well, we did it last summer and didn't have any trouble.

Needless to say the novices turned back far short of their goal. Luckily no harm was done and they learned a good lesson, namely that travel in winter is altogether different from travel in summer. Not that winter hiking is *always* more difficult and slower, but weather and snow conditions really can make or break a winter itinerary. In the summer going down usually takes almost as long as climbing up, but in the winter going down is usually considerably faster than climbing, which may be exceptionally slow. To climb a given peak in the summer may take three hours up and two hours down while in the winter under excellent snow conditions it may take four hours up and an hour and a half down. Under poor conditions it may take even longer. If a summer hiker goes out twelve miles into the backcountry to camp and it rains overnight, the return trip, although wet, may not take very much longer than the approach. If a backcountry skier, on the other hand, makes the same trip and it rains, as it can, rivers and streams may open up, the snow will turn to mush, and the retreat may turn into an epic.

When planning a winter trip, always try to consider how changes in snow and weather conditions may affect you, and try to plan your trip so there are alternative choices you can make if necessary: that is, *leave yourself an out.* All possible alternatives, in addition to your basic itinerary, should be left in the hands of a responsible person who will know when to expect you back, when to start worrying if you're not, and what to do if you don't show up within a certain period of time. Be sure to register at the trailhead when possible, but don't count on this record as your means of salvation should something go wrong. Many of these records are more for statistical purposes, and the groups who establish them cannot afford to go looking for every overdue hiker, especially since many forget to sign out on returning.

FOLLOWING A WINTER TRAIL

Routefinding can be the toughest part of a winter hike, especially in open forests where the "corridor" through the trees may not be readily visible. Finding and following a difficult trail is all part of the winter hiking game, and being successful at it leads to a great feeling of accomplishment. If we wanted it to be easy we'd pave all the trails and run handrails from tree to tree, but that's not why people go hiking.

Winter trails may be coy, but they can't help leaving dozens of tiny clues to lead on the winter trailfinder. I like to divide them up into *The Three T's of trailfinding*: looking at the *terrain*, the *trees*, and the *tread* (or surface of the trail itself). Start out by looking at the

terrain around you. Think about where you are topographically—
in a valley or on a ridge, gentle slope or precipice—then try to confirm this on your map. Does the trail follow the river for two miles
on its left bank and then cross over to the right? Have you gone
about two miles and suddenly can no longer find the trail? Then
think about backing up and looking to see if you might have
missed a stream crossing. It sometimes helps to start thinking in
general terms such as these before getting down on your knees
and sniffing the ground. If, on the other hand, for example, the
trail follows a ridge all the way and you know it, you can quickly
dispense with this step and move on to the next.

Next look at the trees all around you. Are there any prominent
openings that naturally catch your eye? Look for sawed-off
branches, indicating previous trail work. Glance back over your
shoulder to see if there are any blazes pointing in the other direction you may not have spotted. If so, remembering that blazes are
placed to be seen by the hiker approaching, the direction the blaze
is facing may clue you in to an unexpected twist in the trail. If
there is a tree down across the trail, try to imagine what the trail
looked like before the tree fell, then detour 180° around the tree to
see if you can pick up the track coming from beneath it.

Finally, study the tread of the trail itself. Often a faint depres-
sion in the surface of the snow from other parties prior to the last
snowfall can be seen. At other times, even though the snow
appears smooth, a firmness can be felt with one's snowshoes or
skis in the deeper layers of snow.

As soon as you suspect you're off the trail, stop and quickly go
through the three T's. If that fails to show you the way, go back to
the point where you were last *sure* you were on the trail. And remember: trailfinding is a *group* responsibility, not just the person in
front. Everyone should fan out looking for clues. Usually it takes
just a minute before someone reports "I've found it!" and you're
back on your way.

MAPS AND COMPASSES

Maps

A good map is to a winter hiker as a recipe is to a cook. For those not familiar with reading them, maps can be confusing at first, but if you start with the basics that maze of tangles and squiggles will soon be as clear as a picture. For map readers the basic goals are to be able to identify important features such as mountaintops and ridges, valleys and rivers, trails and roads, and to be able to tell the angle of a slope by looking at the map's contour lines.

The best sources of hiking maps for the Northeast are generally the United States Geological Survey (USGS) maps or those put out by some of the local hiking and mountain clubs such as the Adirondack, Green, and Appalachian Mountain Clubs and the New York-New Jersey Trail Conference. Some of the ski touring and snowmobiling organizations also publish maps—these are particularly useful for showing trails that may not appear on the hiking maps. An unprotected paper map will quickly disintegrate in the water and wind, so if your map isn't made out of a waterproof synthetic material it can be protected by sandwiching it between two sheets of clear contact paper or coating it with a liquid waterproofer (available at many outdoor supply stores). Another useful idea is to make several photocopies of the map section in question prior to each trip, and distribute them among all of the party members.

The scale of a map indicates how much it has been shrunk down, that is, how much real distance is represented by a certain distance on the map. Since, for example, there are 63,360 inches in a mile, a map with a scale of 1:63,360 would show one mile of terrain for every inch on the map. (A common standard scale is 1:62,500 which, for most purposes is so close to an inch per mile as to be indistinguishable.) A 1:125,000 scale map would therefore show about two miles to the inch. Metric maps are easy since, as there are 100,000 centimeters in a kilometer, a 1:100,000 scale map shows a kilometer of distance for every centimeter of map.

Roads, trails and summits are fairly easy to spot on a map, but what gives most beginners trouble is to be able to glance at the map and see the terrain features in three dimensions using the contour lines. Each of these lines, which are drawn in on the map, represent a particular altitude. One can imagine them cutting through the ground at evenly spaced intervals, like a series of slices on a pineapple. The closer one gets to the end of the pineapple (or the top of a mountain or hill), the smaller in diameter the slices; so when viewed from above, a summit looks like a series of approximately concentric circles. The distance between every line is known as the "contour interval" and is usually indicated at the edge of the map, e.g., "Contour = 100 ft.," meaning that for every 100 feet of altitude gained or lost the hiker will cross one line on the map. Where the terrain is very steep, the lines will be closely spaced. On a cliff they may even blend together. On some of the more recent maps, and in particular with the help of computers, there may be shading that helps show the contour. This type of map is particularly helpful for novices, as are the "profiles" of trails shown on some maps, i.e., a sideways profile of a particular trail, showing the relative ups and downs. These profiles are generally only found on maps of a particular trail, e.g., the Appalachian Trail maps.

Look at a map of an area you've been to. Notice how the summits appear as a series of gradually decreasing circles, the ridges look like "U's" pointing away from the summits (unless the ridge is a true "knife edge," in which case it may appear as a "V"), and the stream beds look like "V's" pointing toward the summits. Find a summit and identify all of the ridges and valleys leading away from it. Look for a trail that follows a valley, then find one that follows a ridge. Follow a trail that you've hiked before and try to pick out all of the steep sections. With practice, when you look at a map of a place you've never been to before you will be able to quickly pick out the major features and visualize the terrain.

Compasses

As someone who had a hard time getting the lodestone-on-a-cork idea in elementary school I can sympathize with people who find compasses confusing. I figured some of those early explorers spent most of their time emptying the bottles the corks came from, rather than using the compasses, and I decided that group, not the compass users, must have included my ancestors. ("Hey, Orvik, we need another cork for the compass!" "Yah, yah, no problem!") For those of you "cardinally challenged," the important thing to remember about compasses is that they only do two things: they point to the North, and they measure an angle. Keeping these two functions separate in one's mind makes compasses a lot less of a mystery.

Most backpackers use an "orienteering" type compass with a rotating housing on a fixed baseplate. This is far more precise than a cereal box model but without the expense and complexity of the compasses used by surveyors and other professionals. The needle is usually immersed in a liquid so that it will quickly come to a stop without swinging interminably back and forth. There may be a sight to help in picking out distant objects when following a heading (although, for rough sighting, holding the compass at eye level and sighting along the baseplate is usually adequate). Some of the sights use a mirror which, according to a friend of mine, makes the compass doubly useful. "Now," he quips, "not only can the compass tell you where you're lost, but it also lets you know who is lost!"

Unfortunately, when they went and delivered the big magnet up north that attracts all of our compass needles, somebody got lazy and dropped the thing off somewhat short of the true North Pole at a point now known as magnetic north (ran out of corks, I suppose). Consequently, depending on where on the globe we are, magnetic north will appear to be a little to the left or the right of true north. In the Northeast magnetic north is about 15° to the left of true north. This discrepancy is known as the declination. Frankly I'd call it darned poor planning, but they never asked me when they were setting up this system. Rumor has it that magnetic north drifts around a bit (the jokers couldn't even tie it down right!), but not enough to cause any major problems for hikers, at least, as long as you don't run into it.

The problem is that maps show things in terms of true north while our compasses point to magnetic north, and so we have to take declination into account when going from compass bearing to map and vice versa. As an example, suppose you're standing on a summit with your compass pointing directly at another tall mountain several miles away, i.e., in the direction of magnetic north. True north would thus be about 15° to the right of that distant peak. Drats! Suppose there's a peak way off to your right and you want to locate it on your map. Remembering that the compass can only do two things (point to North and measure an angle), first line your compass up so that everything (needle, lines inside the dial, and baseplate) is pointing to magnetic north. Then, to measure the angle between magnetic north and the peak you're looking at, merely rotate the baseplate (keeping the needle and dial in place) until it points at your mystery peak. Now the magnetic bearing can be read from where the numbers on the dial line up with the mark on the baseplate. If you want to convert this magnetic heading into a true bearing all you need to do is subtract the declination: for example, 105° magnetic = 90° true; 300° magnetic = 285° true, and so on. It's easy to forget whether to add or subtract the declination in a given situation, but rather than try to memorize a rule I think it's better to just sit down with the map and work through a series of exercises until it makes sense.

Another and possibly superior solution is to dispense with the North Pole altogether and convert all your maps to magnetic. This is done by drawing in what are known as "magnetic north lines" (some maps already have them). These are parallel lines that traverse the map in the direction of magnetic north. You can easily make them by using a ruler to draw in lines parallel to the magnetic north line which is shown at the edge of the map. Using the same example of a distant peak ahead and to the right, suppose you've found it to be at 38° magnetic. Without magnetic north lines you will have to convert that bearing to 38° - 15° = 23° true, and then find that on the map. With magnetic north lines all you have to do is take the compass set on 38° and line it up on the map so that one end of the direction of travel arrow starts on the point where you are and the arrows inside the housing line up with the magnetic north lines on the map. Now the direction of travel arrow will point right to the peak in question.

Now imagine you want to bushwhack over to that mountain at 38° magnetic. Put your map in your pocket and, with the compass set at 38°, rotate it so that north on the needle lines up with the north lines inside the compass housing. Now the direction of travel arrow will be pointing toward the peak. Rather than walking along holding the compass in front of you and following the needle, you'll find it easier to sight an interesting-looking tree or other distinctive object nearby in the direction you want to go, walk to that, and then sight another object. Another method is to keep the compass bearer behind calling out "left," "right" or "stop" to the person in front who goes on ahead until he or she can barely be seen, at which point the lead person stops and lets the compass bearer catch up. The cycle is repeated until the objective is reached, with everyone taking turns at being compass bearer and leader. This latter method is a good exercise for group compass practice but is rarely used in real-life situations because it is slow.

Another situation that occasionally occurs when you're out on a bushwhack is when you can see two distant points that you recognize and you want to know exactly where you are. If you take a bearing on each of these points and then draw lines on your map along those bearings, passing through the recognizable spots, the point where the two lines intersect will be your approximate position.

Other Aids to Navigation

An altimeter can be a very useful supplement to the compass, especially for those who do a lot of hiking off trails. Altimeters work by measuring the barometric pressure and using the fact that as one ascends, the pressure decreases correspondingly. It must be noted that changes in the barometric pressure due to changes in the weather can confuse the altimeter and cause it to either over or underestimate the altitude. It should be checked and recalibrated every time a known altitude, such as a summit, is reached. Likewise if the altimeter changes say, from 1500 feet above sea level to 1400 feet overnight, that indicates a rise in the barometric pressure, which can be useful in helping to predict the weather. Either that or your tent has slid 100 feet down the mountain, but you could probably figure that out on your own.

For those who lose or forget their compasses, the sun and the stars can be used to find one's way, but it's unusual to be lost in the woods of the northeastern U.S. without a compass and with good enough weather to be able to see the sun or the stars. It is good, though, for winter hikers to be able to recognize the North Star (Polaris) and to know that Orion crosses the southern winter sky, and to realize that the sun rises in the southeast, hits due south about noon, and sets in the southwest. For more information on solar and celestial navigation consult the reference section.

BUSHWHACKING

Fortunately, even in the relatively "developed" northeastern outdoors, there are still many lovely peaks, valleys, and other spots with no trails at all, giving the adventurous winter hiker or skier a nearly infinite variety of places to explore away from the beaten paths. Naturally, before striking out into the unknown one needs a good understanding of the local terrain, a map and compass and the ability to use them, and adequate food and equipment. There are many seasoned bushwhackers around, and many clubs and schools run bushwhacking trips, both of which are an excellent way to get started. To really enjoy poking around in the woods, stepping in holes and getting slapped by branches takes a certain personality, and many backcountry users will find they prefer sticking to trails. A veteran bushwhacker I know once shocked her hiking party by announcing, "You know, I've never liked these bushwhacks—you never know where you're going and you always get poked in the eye!" For those who enjoy it, though, it can be a wonderful way to find solitude and have as close to a true wilderness experience as this part of the country can offer.

That said, I must point out there is a downside to bushwhacking. As many concerned hikers and environmentalists have noted, bushwhacking is not without consequence. Particularly in the relatively small northeastern U.S., with a fairly high number of bushwhackers, popular bushwhacking objectives, e.g., trailless peaks, "hidden" waterfalls, etc., can start to show signs of this use. Broken branches, bits of litter, footprints and, ultimately in some areas, worn unofficial trails known as "herdpaths" may start to develop. As these areas do not have official trails, there is no maintenance, and these herdpaths, usually heading straight up the hillsides, may quickly become badly eroded and ugly, often worse than if there were a trail there to begin with. For these reasons a number of hiking clubs have come out officially opposed to bushwhacking. For a good discussion of this issue, both pro and con, see Laura and Guy Waterman's book *Backwoods Ethics* (2nd edition) listed in the reference section on page 204. If you do bushwhack on occasion, then by all means choose your trips carefully to avoid heavy use areas, keep your party size small, and make as little impact as you possibly can. Think of the woods as a cathedral, and don't knock over the candlesticks.

The late Joe Creager, a well-known and excellent New Hampshire bushwhacker, once put together a list of bushwhacking hints which, with minor editing, are listed below.

ON EQUIPMENT
- Wear glasses in preference to contact lenses.
- A day pack or internal frame pack gets caught on fewer branches than an external frame pack.
- Try to lash skis, axes and crampons onto your pack in a way that they'll avoid low-hanging branches.
- Wear clothing that's durable and resistant to the snow that gets knocked down from evergreen boughs.
- Bring at least two compasses per party, and keep them attached to their owners by a string.

ON SAFETY
- As in any hike, keep track of the person behind you and don't pull away. That way the group stays together.
- Don't step between rocks or logs that could break your leg if you fall. Know what you're stepping on before you commit your weight. If you do fall, try to spin so you land on your pack.
- Be sure everyone in the group knows the proposed route.

ON NAVIGATION AND TERRAIN
- Stay flexible. Swing back and forth to pick up the easiest route, and don't hesitate to follow old logging roads and abandoned trails if they help. Sometimes it may actually be easier to parallel old routes if they're overgrown with saplings.
- Ridges are usually more open than valleys, and it's easier to follow ridges up and streams down due to branching.
- Awareness of the sun's relative position can decrease the need for compass checks.
- Keep assessing your position and look back often to observe your surroundings.

WHITEOUTS

In open, snowy areas such as the alpine or arctic tundra it is not uncommon for fog or blowing snow to come up so thick and so quickly that one becomes trapped in a fuzzy white world where the ground and the sky blend together, and vision may be so limited that one can literally have trouble seeing one's hand in front of one's face. Such "whiteouts" can be completely disorienting and frightening, and even experienced hikers can be thrown way off course or, worse yet, fall over precipices they can't even see. Such was the fate of the legendary Hermann Buhl, who walked off a cornice in a whiteout on Chogolisa in Pakistan. Frequently whiteouts may be short-lived, and if a party has plenty of warm clothing and shelter from the wind they may wait for visibility to improve. If the group decides that it must press on ahead, it is vitally important that no one become separated from the others. On most of the above-treeline trails in the Northeast piles of rocks, known as cairns, have been built to help hikers in low visibility. Sometimes even the next cairn can't be seen, in which case a short length of rope may be invaluable so that one member of the party can range out ahead and signal to the others when he finds the next cairn. Lacking a rope, nylon straps, parachute cord and other pieces of gear may be joined, or a large group may even join hands. If no cairns are present the group may be forced to move by compass alone or use available terrain features like ridges. The usual principles for following a compass bearing also apply in a whiteout, namely that if possible one sights an object and moves to it; but if the visibility is too poor even for that, one may be literally forced to walk along with the compass outstretched in front.

TOTAL NAVIGATION

Ultimately, whether you're in search of a lost trail, taking a compass bearing to a wilderness pond, or lost in the woods and traveling by solar navigation, whatever you do must make sense. It is possible to get turned around 180° and convince yourself that all sorts of ridges and valleys are in places they're not. As Joe Creager also used to like to say, "Do yourself a favor: convince yourself you don't have any sense of direction." By this he meant that navigation is done, as much as humanly possible, by the head, not the heart. You must learn to use the tools of the trade well, and be continuously aware of your position. Travel by knowledge rather than "feel." Whenever you're traveling in the woods, observe your surroundings as well as you can. Look back over your shoulder from time to time; terrain can often look very different on the return trip. Check and double-check all your compass bearings before starting out, and then believe what your compass is telling you. If all else fails and you do lose your way in the Northeast, calmly sit down and think and talk through your position before you continue. In almost every northeastern wilderness area, if you follow a stream downhill you'll come to a trail or a road within a matter of hours or, at the most, one or two days. If you've adequately prepared yourself with clothing and food and left word of your travel plans, it should be nothing more than an adventure until you find your way out or are found.

Moving Ahead

"Let us probe the silent places, let us seek what luck betide us;
Let us journey to a frozen land I know.
There's a whisper on the night-wind, there's a star agleam to guide us,
And the Wild is calling, calling...let us go."
　　　　　　　　　　　—ROBERT SERVICE, "The Call of the Wild"

SNOWSHOEING

The original snowshoes, as far as we can tell, came from the snowy areas of Asia and across the Bering Strait, where they were quickly adopted and improved upon by different groups of native North Americans. The French settling eastern Canada soon heard about these "raquettes de neige," and used them extensively for hunting, trapping and "leisure" activities like footraces. Hikes and other social outings on snowshoes enjoyed tremendous popularity in the 1920s and 30s, and the use of snowshoes for hiking and mountain climbing has continued steadily since then.

　　The most significant change in snowshoe design that has occurred over the past hundred years has been the development of the metal and neoprene shoe, originally called the "Western snowshoe" by some. When these narrow, "hi-tech" snowshoes with their steeply upturned toes first hit the eastern market, one well-known

CARL E. HEILMAN II

Using snowshoes and a skipole to climb a steep slope.

Whee hah! Snowshoes can descend slopes most skiers would never consider.

CARL E. HEILMAN II

and respected winter mountaineering school decided they were "unacceptable" for their students. They worried that the snow-shoes' small size would give inadequate support ("flotation") in deep snows and that the upturned toes wouldn't work for kicking steps up steep slopes. A couple of years later a pair of brothers from out west showed up as students at this school, bringing with them a number of pairs of the radical shoes in various sizes and shapes. They encouraged the instructors and students at the school to compare the new snowshoes with their traditional wood and rawhide ones. For an entire week the group scrambled up, down and across steep mountains and hillsides, until they finally had to concede that the western snowshoes worked just fine in "eastern" conditions. As you may have surmised, the two brothers, Bill and Gene Prater, were both expert snowshoers and snowshoe makers. Not only were their snowshoes quickly accepted but they, too, were invited back to the school, the next time as instructors!

The greatest thing about snowshoes, be they eastern or western, is they work. Try walking a mile or two in knee deep powder without them—it's exhausting. With properly fitted and adjusted snowshoes walking on snow can be a delight.

Frames

The basic components of a snowshoe are the frame, webbing (or decking) that goes inside the frame and provides the flotation, a binding system, and a traction device to help the shoes grip on steep slopes.

Nowhere is the novice snowshoe buyer confronted with so many choices as in trying to decide on the frame. Should I buy wooden or metal snowshoes? Yukon shape or modified bearpaw? How big should they be? are frequently asked questions. The larger a snowshoe is the greater flotation it offers, but the more difficult it becomes to maneuver. For most northeastern hiking and mountain climbing a shoe should be no longer than about three feet and no wider than twelve inches (many beginners will find an eight to ten-inch wide shoe easier to handle). Very small, "feather-weight" snowshoes are becoming increasingly popular, along with the sport of running on snowshoes. Such shoes can be fine on a well-packed trail, but for deep, unconsolidated powder or carrying a heavy pack I would stick to a more traditional size. The best shoes for mountain climbing or walking in thick woods are fairly short and wide, and so the bearpaw, modified bearpaw, and beavertail shapes all work reasonably well. The longer, skinnier types such as the Yukon are better suited to open woods and long, frozen lakes.

White ash has long been the favorite of snowshoe makers for wooden-framed shoes due to its great strength, light weight, and easy bendability. Metal frames, although frequently somewhat lighter, have the main advantages of decreased maintenance and greater strength than wood, although it must be noted that even metal snowshoes can break, especially if they are "bridged" between two objects such as logs or rocks. There are also a number of plastic-framed snowshoes on the market which are cheap and lightweight but in general don't perform as well as wood or metal. Some snowshoers find these to be useful in the springtime when the lower trails are generally free from snow but there may still be some very deep pockets on north facing slopes higher up.

Webbing

Rawhide, the traditional material for snowshoe webbing, requires annual coatings with varnish or polyurethane to keep it from soaking up water. (On very wet days, it still will.) When rawhide webbing becomes wet it stretches like soggy spaghetti, and huge clumps of snow stick to it like cement. Neoprene, a type of nylon coated with rubber, has largely taken the place of rawhide even in many traditional wooden frames. Some manufacturers use other synthetics like urethane. For the purists, however, rawhide lacing does make for a beautiful and, under most conditions, perfectly functional snowshoe.

(Opposite) The old and the new: (a) in front is a traditional wood and rawhide snowshoe. The metal/neoprene shoe in the back is smaller and has a sharply upturned toe. Close-up (b) of a metal/neoprene "western" snowshoe.

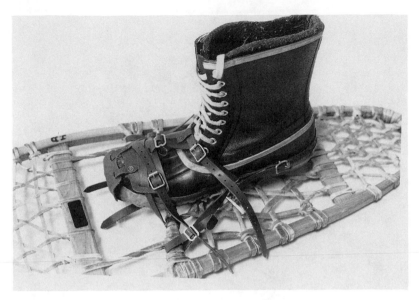

"Alphabet" binding, showing the toe cup, heel and instep straps.

Bindings

The role of a snowshoe binding is to keep the boot firmly attached to the shoe with a minimum of sideplay, while at the same time allowing it to "hinge" freely. This means that the toe of the shoe rises up as you pick up your foot, thereby allowing it to come up out of the shoeprint without catching on the snow. This hinging should occur without any conscious effort on the part of the snowshoer, so that walking on snowshoes becomes a fluid and natural act.

One of the earliest and simplest bindings was made by wrapping a length of cord or wicking material from a kerosene lamp over the toe of the boot, under the toe cord of the shoe and around the ankle, and finally tying across the top of the foot. These "lampwick" bindings, when properly tied, are surprisingly secure and can be used as an emergency replacement. Another "old-fashioned" binding that's very popular among professional loggers is the "inner tube" binding. Made from a single piece of rubber, these bindings are very easy to put on and take off, and quite adequate for gentle woods walking. They lack the lateral stability necessary for traveling heavily laden over difficult terrain, however.

After the lampwick and inner tube bindings come a number of increasingly complex leather or neoprene models, most of which share three major components: a toe strap or toe cup that positions the ball of the foot over the toe cord, to keep it from sliding forward on downhills; a heel strap, passing behind the boot heel to keep it from sliding backwards on uphills; and an instep strap which holds the heel strap in place and adds to the overall lateral stability of the shoe. These types of bindings are called by a variety of letter names such as "H," "F," and "K," and so henceforth I'll refer to them as "alphabet bindings." The advantage of a closed-in toe cup is that it keeps the boot from slipping forward better than a simple toe strap; but it does cover up the toe of the boot sole, which with the open-toed bindings can sometimes be kicked into hard snow to give extra grip. With a good traction device, however, this use of the boot toe is unnecessary.

With the arrival of the metal and neoprene shoes came yet a third major type of binding, as different from the rest as lampwicks from alphabet bindings. In all the earlier bindings the boot hinged directly on the toe cord of the shoe so that any play in the cord would result in sideways play of the boot. In the newest type of bindings, made popular by the Sherpa® snowshoe company (and hence sometimes collectively referred to as "Sherpa bindings"), a rigid metal rod instead of a cord traverses the shoe just behind the toe hole. The boot is held in a neoprene or plastic cup, on the bottom of which are metal hinges or fasteners that attach to the metal rod. In this way the moving parts of the snowshoe are metal on metal rather than boot on flexible toe cord, which makes for a more secure and durable binding.

Whichever type of binding is used, the basics of adjustment are the same. Begin by positioning the boot in the toe cup so that the tip of the toe sits in the middle of the toe hole with the ball of the foot over or just behind the toe cord or rod. Then tighten the toe cup (or strap). Next do the heel strap, and last, fasten the instep strap (if there is one). With most bindings one or two straps may be left in a "preset" position so only one strap need be done and undone when getting in and out of the snowshoe. In the alphabet bindings the toe and heel straps are left in place so only the instep strap need be unfas-

Young snowshoer crossing a stream.

CARL E. HEILMAN II

tened, while with the Sherpa-type bindings the heel strap can be left in place, and the toe cup is unlaced for easy exit.

With some of the Sherpa-type bindings there is a tendency for the heel strap to slip off on the downhills. This is because no matter how tight one makes things, it is almost impossible to take out all of the play from the system, and hiking downhill causes a slight forward shift of the boot which loosens the heel strap. Being meticulous about tightening the bindings can sometimes remedy the problem, but more often than not some further ingenuity is required. One solution is to make an instep strap similar to the one found on the alphabet bindings, but this can complicate certain lacing systems considerably. Another trick that works well is to sew a loop of Velcro™ material to the lower rear edge of each of one's gaiters, which is then fastened around the heel strap to hold it in place.

Traction Devices

Using snowshoes without crampons is like driving a car in the winter with summer tires on. For enjoyable snowshoeing on anything but level ground a good crampon or similar traction device is nearly essential. Most of the metal-framed snowshoes come with a crampon as part of the binding system whereas with most of the wooden shoes crampons must be added by the owner. The most common way of doing this is to lash either a boot instep crampon or part of an old regular boot crampon to the bottom of the snowshoe just behind the toe hole, using wire or parachute cord. Wire is easier to tighten, but can cut through the snowshoe lacing in time. The vertical posts of the crampon can either be sawn off with a hacksaw or heated and bent flat (this leaves a little more to tie to) to keep them from sticking up into the webbing. The crampons are then left on the snowshoes at all times. They won't be noticed in soft powder yet will be right there where they're needed for any crusty or icy patches. With metal-framed snowshoes err on the side of the heavier crampons if there's a choice. A number of shoes come with very flimsy serrated aluminum "potato scraper" crampons that have a tendency to break and not grip very well. The crampons with longer, sturdier teeth such as the Tucker Claw® are superior.

CARL E. HEILMAN II

Kicking steps on the Adirondack's Algonquin.

CARL E. HEILMAN II

A sitting glissade on snowshoes.

Snowshoeing Technique

So how do they work, anyway? Some authors have said, "You just strap on the suckers and walk." This is true to a point, however snowshoeing is one of those skills where the basics are simple but the fine points are subtle. I had this driven home to me one year while leading a group of "advanced" winter backpacking students on a week-long trip in the mountains. During the previous two winters there had been little snow, therefore most of the students were skilled at using crampons and hiking on slippery ground, but very few of them had done any serious snowshoeing. The second day out we encountered two feet of fresh powder and, although the incline was moderate, most of them did so much slipping, sliding and falling that they were soon exhausted and we only made two and a half miles that day. This is not to belittle their accomplishments, but rather to point out that with snowshoeing, there can be more than meets the eye.

On the flats it is true that it's mostly a matter of putting one foot in front of the other. The snowshoes overlap slightly in mid-stride, the top one gliding over the bottom one so that the snowshoer *doesn't* have to walk like a duck.

As the grade steepens, balance becomes more and more critical. Rather than bull his way up forcefully, the good snowshoer stalks uphill like a cat on the prowl, placing each foot precisely and carefully. Occasionally he may choose to stamp a shoe vigorously downwards to sink in his crampons or pack out a step, but he always tries to avoid flailing away helplessly like a cartoon character winding up for a getaway. A good snowshoer, as with any physical task, is smooth and precise, with an economy of extraneous movements.

When ordinary headfirst methods no longer work, the snowshoer is forced to resort to more creative techniques, i.e., cunning and trickery. On uneven inclines (most northeastern trails!) it is important to "pick out the pockets", that is, to study the slope for little depressions where one can get a step that is less steep than its surroundings. This is most commonly on top of a rock, or a tree root. Learn to read the trail like a whitewater canoeist reads rapids, and seek out the easiest line. On smooth, unbroken snow one can either ascend by a series of rising traverses (i.e., zig-zag), which is easier with western snowshoes, or "kick steps" in the slope, a technique more suited to flat-toed shoes. In order to kick step the snowshoer must fool the snowshoe's natural tendency to hinge so that the toe of the shoe, rather than tipping up, actually dips *down* as the foot is brought forward. In this way the shoe actually sinks into the slope at a slight downward angle. Then when the shoe is stepped up upon, the weight of the snowshoer will cause it to level out. To do this takes a snap of the lower leg, sort of like kicking a ball. One's companions must be careful when following behind someone who's kicking steps, to avoid receiving any unsolicited "nose jobs."

To go downhill on snowshoes is simpler: walk straight ahead. It generally helps to sit back a little, to keep the snowshoe toes from catching in the snow and causing a tumble. On very steep slopes it may be possible to get one's snowshoes to slide almost like skiing, a technique known as *glissading*. Sit back on your tails, brace yourself with ice axe or ski poles, and enjoy the ride!

Maintenance and Repair

Metal and neoprene snowshoes are practically maintenance free and rarely break, but they still should be inspected periodically for buckles pulling apart, crampons loosening and other signs of wear and tear. The plastic lacing used on many of the metal snowshoes to hold on the decking can be a weak point, particularly if one is forced to do any snowshoeing on rocky stretches. What happens is the lacing wears through on the underside of the shoe where it wraps around the frame, and unless this area is inspected from time to time the lacing can break. If it does break, it can usually be spliced back together with a small C-shaped metal clip and pair of pliers to crimp it. Ask your local snowshoe dealer for some spares. Failing that, many hardware stores carry suitable alternatives, such as connecters for various types of cable or wires. In time the neoprene or nylon straps on some of the binding systems will fray. If caught early, these ragged fibers can be carefully melted back with a candle or torch. Wooden shoes and rawhide lacings should be coated annually with varnish or polyurethane to protect them from water damage. Broken rawhide webbing may be repaired by soaking the shoe in a tub of water for one or two days, which makes it soft enough to splice in new pieces of rawhide. If a frame breaks in the field it can be splinted with sticks held in place by parachute cord or the ubiquitous duct tape.

SKIING

"I had never gone so fast before in my life—not even on a train—and that is what I liked about it. Climbing was slow and skiing so fast ... Major White suggested that some day I might find it useful in my mountaineering." —TENZING NORGAY, *Tiger of the Snows*

Tenzing was not alone—in a similar way many die-hard hikers have discovered skiing to be a useful and enjoyable addition to their backcountry skills. The expensive and fashionable lift-serviced skiing we've all come to know is a fairly recent development. For thousands of years prior to the construction of the first ski tows, people were using skis as a self-propelled way of traveling about snowy places in winter. The earliest known ski, coming from a Swedish bog (don't ask me why they were skiing in bogs), dates from about 2500 B.C., and boy, did it need a tuneup. When large numbers of Scandinavians emigrated to the U.S. in the 1800s they brought this well-developed skill with them, and soon many local ski organizations sprang up, like the Nansen Ski Club in Berlin, New Hampshire, which has been in existence since before the turn of the century.

During the academic year of 1909–1910, an undergraduate student at Dartmouth College named Fred Harris started the famous Dartmouth Outing Club, and in 1911 they held their first winter carnival. Soon, scores of Dartmouth-trained skiers fanned out all over the Northeast, and skiing was here to stay. At that time most of the skiers stuck either to open lowland hillsides or trails specifically cut for skiing, but some of the more adventurous soon discovered their skis could indeed take them to a fair number of places visited previously in winter only on snowshoes. Miriam Underhill and friends made a number of remarkable ski ascents (and descents) in the 1920s on mountains like Washington (NH) and Katahdin (ME).

In the 1930s the forerunners of downhill, or alpine, skiing as we know it came of age in America. In the 1932 Olympics at Lake Placid the slalom and downhill skiing events were first introduced, and in 1934 the first ski tow in the United States was built in Woodstock, Vermont. As skiers flocked to the downhill slopes with their rope tows, chair lifts and cable cars, backcountry or cross-country skiing was largely forgotten.

Then, in the 1970s, some interesting things happened. One was that a veritable "fitness craze" swept the country. Sales of running shoes skyrocketed. "Fitness centers" sprang up in towns too small for shopping centers, while medical studies from Europe showed cross-country skiing (which hadn't been forgotten there) was one of the finest total body conditioners. Gasoline prices also soared to over a dollar per gallon, and prices of lift tickets at the downhill areas crept up to twenty dollars per day and kept going. To top it all off, an underdog American named Bill Koch from Putney, Vermont, won a silver medal in cross-country skiing in the 1976 winter Olympics, and cross-country skiing was back with a passion. Just as the downhill areas had sprung up all over the Northeast, so did cross-country centers with ski schools, groomed trails, cafeterias—in many ways the very things that disgruntled downhillers had been trying to escape.

As the more adventurous skiers had done in the twenties, backcountry skiers of the 1970s and '80s began to strike out on their own, skiing deep into the backcountry, camping, and climbing up mountains. In response to the need for increased traction to make some of the steeper ascents, climbing skins were reborn, and to help negotiate difficult downhills the telemark turn, named after its birthplace in Norway, was revived. Watching the modern backcountry skier laboring uphill with climbing skins, threading through the brush on a bushwhack, or gliding downhill in a series of beautiful turns, we can take comfort in the fact that backcountry skiing, like everything else, has finally come full circle, back to its origins.

Skis

Just about every conceivable length, width, and shape of ski has been used for backcountry skiing at one time or another. Nowadays most fit into one of three general types: touring; backcountry/telemark; or mountaineering/alpine touring.

This method of strapping skis to a pack works well for open trails, but beware of branches in heavily wooded areas.

Touring skis are narrow and lightweight, without metal edges (about 42-52mm wide and up to about four pounds per pair). They can be used on easy to moderate backcountry trips, depending on the skier's ability and the loads carried.

Backcountry/telemark skis are wider (usually 50–70mm), weigh between four and six pounds per pair, and have metal edges for improved control on hard or icy snow. To help them turn better than traditional cross-country skis they incorporate some of the features found in downhill skis. Within this category there are both single- and double-camber models.

Camber refers to the amount of curve of the ski when viewed from the side. A single-camber ski, as are downhill skis today, is relatively flat, which makes it easier to turn. If you hold a pair of single-cambered skis bottom to bottom, they will nearly touch even in the middle. A double-camber ski, as are most of the touring models, has a greater curve, which provides a "pocket" under the foot area for waxing. In this way, when the skier presses down hard, e.g., to kick and glide, the wax is pressed down into the snow to provide grip. When the skier is gliding, however, and not pressing down so hard, the wax pocket holds the wax up more out of the snow, so the ski can slide on its slipperier-waxed tip and tail sections. If you hold up a pair of double-camber skis base to base, you can usually fit your hand between them under the foot sections. Which camber to get, single or double, depends on the skiing you do. For skiing in the woods, with lots of little ups and downs, double-cambered skis are better for their better waxability and kicking and gliding. For climbing up mountains and skiing back down, single-cambered skis with climbing skins for the ascents will make for easier turning on the way down.

Mountaineering/alpine touring skis are basically downhill skis fitted with alpine-touring or "randonnée" bindings. These hinged bindings hold a rigid plastic ski or climbing boot and can be used in either a hinged position for climbing, or locked down flat on the ski for doing parallel turns on the descent.

Most of these skis are made from a mixture of fiberglass and wood. All-wood skis are aesthetically pleasing and hold waxes well, but they are more easily broken than fiberglass and require more maintenance. Fiberglass is incorporated into skis in a number of ways, beginning with single reinforcing strips, then as a sandwich with a layer of fiberglass on both bottom and top, and finally as a box that completely envelops a wood or synthetic core (known as "torsion-box construction").

All wooden skis depend on waxes to be able to grip when they're pushed upon and glide when the pressure is released. Synthetic skis may be designed either to use waxes or they may be "waxless." The simplest waxless skis have a pattern carved into the bottom that grips in one direction and glides in the other (as in the

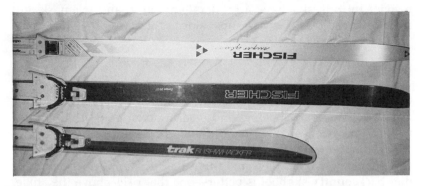

Bottom to top: Trak Bushwhacker, Telemark Backcountry (metal edges), Recreational Citizen Racing Ski.

"fishscale" design). Some of the most recent waxless designs are smooth to the touch yet have microscopic irregularities of one kind or another that allow them to grip. At present, a well-waxed ski will usually out-perform a waxless ski in most stable conditions, but in the fickle Northeast, where snow conditions change frequently, the savings in time and trouble make waxless skis very popular. This is especially true in the springtime, when one can go from ice to slush to ice again in a matter of minutes. Every spring I swear I'll buy waxless, and the following December or January, surrounded by beautiful powder, I quickly forget.

For many years it has been said that a ski should reach from the floor to the wrist of the skier's upheld arm. This is still a reasonable guide; but for those who like to ski down difficult slopes a somewhat shorter ski will be easier to turn, while for those who prefer to carry heavier packs on gentler trails the increased flotation and stability of a longer ski may be desirable. Likewise for two skiers of similar height, the heavier or more aggressive skier will usually want a slightly longer ski. Any good ski shop employee will be able to help you arrive at the best length for you.

In addition to the camber, as previously described, another feature that determines how easily a ski turns is its *sidecut*. Sidecut refers to the way the middle part of a ski is narrower than the tip and tail sections, so that when it's placed on edge it wants to turn on its own. Cross-country racing skis have little if any, while heavier touring skis have a moderate amount, and telemark and alpine touring skis have the most sidecut of all.

Boots

Oh, for the perfect winter boot that would work equally well for hiking, skiing, snowshoeing, and wearing crampons! With lighter weight touring gear most people will choose fairly light, single-weight boots, which are often adequate for day trips in moderate conditions. For colder days and multi-day trips a warmer and sturdier backcountry ski boot is better—one that rises above the ankle, with insulated padding inside and a thicker, stiffer sole. If they're bought roomy enough to accommodate two or three pairs of socks they can be quite warm, especially if combined with an insulated supergaiter. For maximum warmth and support there are also double ski boots, similar to double mountaineering boots, with a soft, insulated inner boot and a stiffer, leather or plastic outer boot. Over the past several years boots for telemarking, influenced no

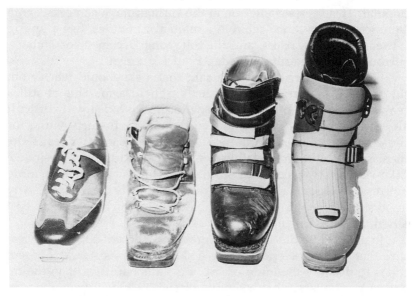

Cross-country ski boots may range from the lightweight touring shoe on the left to the hi-tech plastic ski mountaineering boot on the right.

doubt by downhill skiing technology, have become increasingly sophisticated. For added support and control over a simple leather boot, plastic buckles, particularly above the ankle, are often seen, while for the very serious telemark skiers and racers, all-plastic boots, similar to downhill boots except for the flex at the ankles, are the rage. Some people use these plastic ski boots with their crampons or snowshoes as well, making them about the closest thing going to an all-around winter backcountry boot.

Bindings

Between the years 1910 and 1915 Norway's Lauritz Bergendahl went undefeated in the prestigious 50-kilometer Holmenkollen race. His secret? Among other things, the three-pin ski binding he invented, the most popular binding in ski touring today. Bergendahl understood that in order to get the most efficient power and speed from a ski, the heel of the boot must be free to lift up. The older cable bindings in use at the time gave somewhat greater stability on the downhills but were definitely slower on the uphills and flats. In the three-pin binding the toe section of the boot has three holes drilled partway up into the sole, into which fit the three vertical steel pins of the binding. The boot is clamped down onto those three pins by a metal bail that fits across the top of the sole, where it protrudes in front of the boot a centimeter or two. Aficionados of this type of binding are sometimes referred to (usually affectionately) as "pinheads."

Fortunately the old cable bindings were not completely forgotten. In this type of binding the toe of the boot is slotted into a "toe iron" similar, in a sense, to the toe cup of a snowshoe binding, only made of metal. A springy steel cable passing behind the heel of the boot is then tightened by a lever, which brings the boot forward to lock it into the toe iron. This type of binding was abandoned by downhill skiers about thirty years ago in favor of bindings that would release the skier's boot in the event of a fall. These "safety bindings" resulted in a dramatic reduction in the number of broken legs at the downhill slopes. For backcountry skiing, however, the modern cable binding provides a greater measure of control than three-pin bindings, is easier on boot soles, and with the slower speeds, lighter skis and softer boots of backcountry skiing,

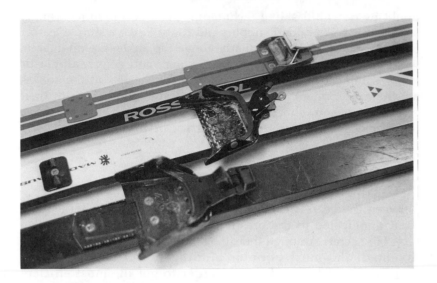

Three different approaches to back-country ski gear: on top is a light touring ski with a toe clamp binding; in the middle a medium-weight touring ski with a traditional three-pin binding, and on the bottom a heavy, metal-edged telemark/ mountaineering ski, with a heavy-duty three-pin "telemark" binding.

leg injuries with this type of binding are relatively rare. For those who are worried, however, there are now some release mechanisms for backcountry skis, too. These are typically a release plate and mechanism which is bought separately and mounted to the ski, onto which the binding (either cable or three-pin) is then mounted. It is very likely this type of system will grow in popularity as more and more downhill-trained skiers grow weary of lift-lines, and take to the hills on their own.

A third type of binding which has been popular with European ski mountaineers for some time is the hinged plate (a.k.a alpine touring or randonnée) design, in which the boot is mounted on a rigid metal plate which is then attached to the ski by an actual hinge. For downhill runs and a rigidity and control similar to that found with downhill ski bindings the plate can be locked down. Similar but less rigid plate type bindings such as the Berwin binding use a flexible plastic plate under the boot. One of the nice things about these types of binding is that they allow for the use of just about any kind of boot.

After about seventy years of racing on essentially the same Bergendahl three-pin cross-country bindings, the industry has come up with several new designs that involve a short metal rod at the toe of the boot which is locked into the binding toepiece. So far these are very good for cross-country touring and racing, but have not supplanted three-pin bindings for most backcountry use.

Poles

Bamboo ski poles have gone the way of the deerskin sleeping bag and have been replaced by the far stronger metal and fiberglass ones. Since they are used for propulsion as well as for balance, cross-country poles must be longer than their downhill counterparts and generally should come up close to the skier's armpits. For those who do primarily "climb up, ski down" type of skiing a shorter pole, of intermediate length, is advisable. The extra length of touring poles can be cumbersome on downhills, however, and so for long descents many skiers "choke up" on their poles. Another option, for those who do a lot of backcountry downhill, is to buy adjustable ski poles. Some of these can be converted to emergency avalanche probes, which makes them especially popular in the vast, open snowfields out west. For extremely steep ski descents there are even poles with picks on the handles, to self-arrest in the event of a fall.

Ski pole baskets, which keep the poles from sinking too deeply into the snow, come in a variety of shapes from the tiny racer's "sharkfin" to large (6" plus) "powder baskets." For general

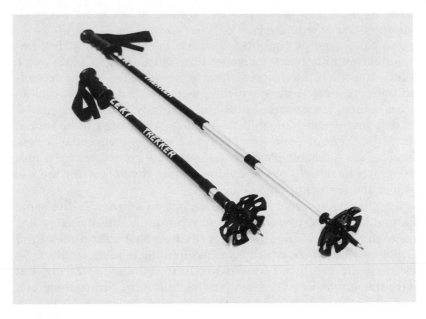

Adjustable ski poles are a help for skiers who do a lot of steep uphills and downhills.

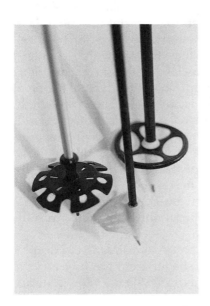

Three types of ski pole baskets: the traditional "crossed circle," the racer's "sharkfin," and the "snowflake" design (which is less apt to hang up on branches than the crossed circle).

backcountry use most people find an intermediate-sized basket from three and three-quarter to four and one-half inches in diameter to be the best, as the sharkfins tend to dive out of sight in soft powder and the powder baskets are quite heavy (and, alas, rarely needed in the Northeast!). The traditional crossed circle shape is still very popular; there are a few other shapes such as the snowflake and triangle that are slightly less apt to snag on branches.

Skins and Climbers

The original climbing skins were just that, strips of animal skin (generally seal) strapped to the ski bottoms with the hairs angled backwards. Modern skins are synthetic but work the same way, having either a hairlike material or a pattern cut into plastic. They may attach either with buckles and straps (which are quicker and easier but more prone to slip off) or with a reusable sticky glue, which works best on a clean, unwaxed ski. Most skins extend the entire length of the ski, but there are also some short skins, known as "kicker skins" that only cover the middle third of the ski. These are lightweight, and give plenty of grip for many moderate uphills.

To ascend using skins, the skis are pointed straight uphill and slid just as if one were performing a shuffling stride on the flat. Try not to lift the skis, as this takes more energy and can lead to sore muscles and tendons. Resist also the temptation to herringbone ('And lead us not into herringboning...'), as this may cause the skins to slip off, and rely on your legs not your arms. You'll be amazed at the slopes you can climb.

Skins can also be left on for downhills, either if more uphills are soon to follow and taking them off and putting them on again wouldn't be worth it, or to help hold the skier's speed in check on a difficult slope. For truly terrifying descents some skiers have even been known to put their skins on their skis *backwards* (this may require duct tape and a good psychiatric evaluation)! Before trying to ski downhill with skins on, though, remember that the skins will greatly reduce the skis' abilities to edge and turn.

To get the maximum life out of your climbing skins, be sure to unpack and hang them up to dry between every trip.

It took me about two seasons of glopping on extra heavy wax for steep uphills and a lot of herringboning before I finally broke down and bought a pair of skins. Since then I have effortlessly passed numerous skiers bogged down in deep, heavy powder, or slipping and sliding on crust. They are worth every penny.

Repairs

Trying to ski with a broken tip is like trying to ride a bike with flat tires. For a few dollars one can buy a good plastic or metal emergency tip that will slide over the broken end of the ski and allow the skier to make it out to the road without a series of maddening "face plants." At least one per party should be brought on every trip. It is also possible to splint a broken tip with a sturdy piece of sapling and some parachute cord or tape. In a pinch a leather mitten can be stuffed over the tip and tied or taped in place, but the performance will be marginal at best. A more difficult problem occurs when a ski breaks in the middle, which is probably more common with fiberglass skis (wood tends to break at the tip). In some cases the break can be partially held together with tape, but don't count on it. Broken ski poles are more easily mended, especially if they have a hollow core, in which case a strong green sapling just big enough to fit inside can be cut and used as an internal splint with the fragmented ends of the pole taped or hose-clamped around it. With solid core poles three or four similar splints can be applied to the outside of the pole and taped or clamped. Binding failures usually consist of either losing their bales, or pulling out of the ski (a.k.a "total binding blowout"). The latter event is most unsettling, especially when it occurs halfway down "Devil's Drop." Some types of three-pin bindings are notorious for losing their bails and so an extra should be carried, as well as any screwdrivers or other tools that might be needed for a particular set of bindings. Total binding blowout can usually be fixed by screwing them back on with a dab of epoxy glue in the hole and a pinch of steel wool, duct tape, or other available filler. If *you're* still in one piece, that is.

Waxing

Cold, newfallen snow crystals are very sharp, and as they age become rounder and smoother. A ski wax must be of the right consistency to allow the snow crystals to penetrate it when the skier is pushing down on the ski (for grip), but then not penetrate when the ski needs to glide. Thus for sharp, newfallen snow crystals a very hard wax is needed; as the snow ages, softer and softer waxes are used. If a wax is too hard for the given conditions it will slip and slide very well, too well, in fact, so that the skier can't get any "kick." If the wax is too soft, however, the kick will be great but the glide will be lacking.

The harder waxes come in short, candle-shaped sticks that are rubbed on the ski bottom in a thin layer which is then smoothed out with a cork, a glove, or even a bare hand. The softest of waxes, known as klisters, are squeezed from a tube like toothpaste. Klisters, often used in the spring, are for older snows, from slush to refrozen ice, and are applied by squeezing a thin bead on the ski bottom and smoothing it out with a plastic spatula. Waxes come in different colors to denote a certain temperature range for which the wax is designed. Keep in mind that differences in the way the wax is applied, the type of ski being used, and the characteristics of the individual skier all have an effect on how a particular wax works. A good general rule of thumb is if it's so cold you can't make a snowball at all, use green wax. If you can, but it falls apart when you throw it, use blue, and if it sticks together well, use red. Since synthetic-bottomed skis lose their wax more quickly than wooden ones many skiers use special "binder" waxes as a first coat to help hold the waxes on or, at home, use a hot iron to melt in the first coat, so-called "hot waxing." There are even some miniature torches that can be brought along to hot wax on the trail. Do not, I repeat, do not try to wax skis over a camp stove! How do I know this? Don't ask.

When the ski is in a gliding position, because of its camber it rests primarily on its tip and tail sections. For this reason the "tips and tails" of a ski should be waxed with a harder "glider" wax, while the section of the ski directly underfoot (a.k.a "wax pocket") takes a stickier "kicker" wax. For example, one may wax the entire ski with a base coat of "special green" wax (fairly hard) and then add an 18 or so-inch kicker section of green wax (one step softer than special green). Another general rule of thumb is softer waxes can be applied over harder ones, but not the other way around. That said, it's therefore best to err on the side of starting out with a too-hard wax and having to add some softer wax on top of it rather than having to scrape off the soft wax and start over again.

There are three ways to remove old waxes: heat, chemicals, and elbow grease. To use heat, the wax is carefully melted with a propane torch and wiped off with a rag. This method cannot be recommended for synthetic-bottomed skis because of their tendency to melt, although some skiers get away with it if they do it very gingerly. In the elbow-grease method a plastic or steel scraper is used to lift off the bulk of the wax. Both of these methods leave a thin film of wax on the ski which may or may not be desirable as a binder, depending on the conditions and the subsequent wax to be used. If this film is to be removed entirely, a solvent such as paint-thinner or a commercially-prepared ski wax remover will make short work of it.

Ski Technique

It is beyond the scope of this book to give a detailed explanation of all backcountry ski techniques, but I will try to hit some of the highlights. For more instruction the reader is urged to consult some of the very fine books on ski technique in the references and, of course, to obtain good, personal attention from a skilled teacher.

On the Flats. Many elementary explanations of the skier's diagonal stride state "It's as easy as walking." This may be true, but remember most of us took a good year to learn the basics of that! Walking on skis is like walking, but if all we wanted to do on our skis was walk, we'd stick to snowshoes. We want to *slide!*

Diagonal striding is more like riding a scooter (or skateboard) alternating feet as you go—one foot pushes back hard while the other stretches out front for as long as it can before switching and pushing off onto the other foot. In order to make the kicking foot grab it must not simply be pushed backwards. Rather it must be forced *down* into the snow and backwards. The more weight the skier can balance over the kicking ski, the better it grips. In this way the skier must subtly shift weight from side to side with each stride. This is difficult at first, but as one's balance improves it gets easier.

The poles work in synchrony with the *opposite* leg, that is the left arm goes ahead with the right leg, and vice versa. This is comfortable and natural, just like walking. One's arms should be basically straight, so that the power of poling comes from the shoulders and back, not just the upper arm muscles. If the pole strap is correctly adjusted it will be possible to hold onto the poles between your thumb and index finger, gripping them lightly and allowing the strap to do the work.

The additional weight of a pack will press one's skis more firmly into the snow, thereby increasing the kick and decreasing glide. This means that often times a harder wax may be used than would be right for an unladen skier. The difference in one's center of gravity due to a pack can also be startling, especially on the first good downhill or dip. Packing the weightier items somewhat lower down in the pack will help.

Going Up. Forsaking the gentler valley trails and striking out for the summits tests even the strongest of skiers. Skis have a nasty tendency to kick out backwards at the most inopportune times, and the skier's arms are asked to take an increasing share of the load. It is important to look for just the right amount of forward lean—too far back and the arms give out, too far forward and the skis start to slip. Sometimes "slapping" one's skis down hard on the snow will make the wax grip better. For short, steeper sections a quick sidestep or herringbone will do the trick, but for long, sustained uphills one will be forced to add more or softer wax or switch to climbing skins.

Going Down. Here's where skis really earn their keep, at the start of a long, powdery downhill. On gentle grades the skier may want to push a little by "double poling" (p. 177), but most of the time, on narrow, steep mountain trails, the backcountry skier wants anything but to go faster. The first thing to realize is that it's no disgrace to walk down a section (staying off to the side, of course, so as not to leave dangerous "post-holes" that might cause other skiers to fall). Breaking a leg at a downhill ski area is bad enough; it's worse in the backcountry. Another option is to put on your climbing skins, which will provide considerable braking power. Some of the 1920s and 30s skiers developed a wide array of ways of using their ski poles as a brake—dragged out to the side like a rudder behind one knee or even between both legs. (For some unknown reason the line of skiers using this latter technique has mysteriously failed to bear children...) At other times the skier is forced to go from tree to tree in a desperate and environmentally detrimental "glide and lunge" pattern. Strongly consider eye protection

For short, steeper sections a quick herringbone will do the trick.

The diagonal stride.

Double poling.

such as glasses or goggles, for any woody descents. Ultimately, as the trail opens up and flattens somewhat and the skier's courage blossoms forth, these timid techniques are cast by the wayside. The once-floundering backcountry skier who's starting to wonder if maybe he should have brought snowshoes after all points his skis downhill and starts to turn them in a series of beautiful arcs. Suddenly, it's all been worthwhile.

Turning. Most downhill skiers learn to turn their skis in a gradual progression from snowplow (or wedge) to stem to parallel turns, although some skiers start out with short skis and learn parallel turns right away. All of these and more can be done on cross-country skis, but since the cross-country skier's equipment is much less rigid than the downhiller's and his heels aren't held down, there's a tendency for beginning cross-country skiers to fall forward on downhills when they hit a slight bump or slow patch of snow. Snowplow turns help prevent this tendency to fall forward and so, unfortunately, many backcountry skiers never progress beyond the snowplow turn, which is somewhat awkward and tiring (albeit effective).

In the *snowplow* position, as shown in the photo, the skier's legs are spread and his skis are angled toward one another in a wedge or V-shape. His knees are bent and his skis are tilted so that they rest on their inner edges, which dig in and provide the braking power. The more he spreads his legs and the harder he digs in his edges the more he slows down. To turn in this position all he needs do is press harder on one leg than the other; for example, to turn to the right he presses hard on his left ski.

The *step turn* is very useful for quick changes in direction, and easy to do. Starting with both skis together and parallel, the leading ski (right for a right turn and left for a left) is merely picked up, angled in the desired direction and put back down on the snow. To avoid going into a split, just as the lead ski is put down, the trailing ski is picked up and brought parallel once again with the lead ski. In this way the skier does a little shuffle or hop, which may be repeated several times if necessary until the turn is completed.

Parallel turns on cross-country skis are essentially the same as on downhill skis; however, the front-to-back balance is tricky and most skiers find they must sit back a little to avoid falling forwards. This is not a turn for beginners unless they are already accomplished downhill skiers.

A snowplow (or wedge) turn to the right.

The *telemark turn* is graceful, efficient, and perfectly suited to free heel bindings. The easiest way for beginners to learn to telemark is by taking a few lessons on gentle, well-groomed snow, such as at a downhill ski area's beginner slope. It takes a little time to catch on, but the budding telemarker shouldn't despair as it usually "clicks" into place after several attempts. Stiffer boots and metal-edged skis make the learning somewhat easier, although even racing skis can be used in powder or packed powder snow.

To begin to learn to telemark, imagine you're riding a bicycle, but instead of front and back wheels you have front and back skis. The front ski does the turning and the back ski follows behind. If you turn very slowly you'll tend to tip over, but pick up a little speed and the centrifugal force of the turn will allow you to lean inwards and stay in balance.

The basic foundation for the turn is the "telemark position." It's the way that ski jumpers land, almost as kneeling on one knee without quite touching the back knee down, so that most of the weight is still held by the front leg (p. 181). The turn itself can be broken down into three phases: the *set-up phase*, the *weight shift* into

Some of the early skiers developed a wide array of ways of using their ski poles as a brake.

the telemark position, and the *recovery phase*. It's a good idea to start out practicing the telemark position without trying to turn. Glide down a smooth, gentle slope in the telemark stance. Try it a few times with one leg forward until that becomes comfortable, and then do it with the other leg in front. Then glide down a slope alternating legs. To set up a turn to the right, the left leg will be out in front, and it must be angled slightly to the right. The greater the angle, the sharper the turn, but remember, the turn should be like the arc of a bicycle turn—the front ski should "carve" a path for the back one. If you are angling it so much that it skids like a snowplow, that's too much. If you drop into the telemark position and then try to turn the front ski, you'll find that it sticks because you've got too much weight on it, so the trick of setting up a telemark turn is to angle the front ski *as it's gliding forward*, before you shift your weight onto it.

Starting with your feet together, you slide the left ski forward, angling it slightly as you do, to a point where your left foot is just behind the tip of your right ski. *Then* you drop your weight forward onto that angled front ski and *voilà!* you start turning.

To come out of the turn you simply bring your legs back together and stand up. If you keep on moving through this neutral position so that your right ski now angles and slides forward, you will all of a sudden be ready for a turn to the left. Eventually you'll develop a rhythm, a gentle upward and downward bobbing as you lean first one way then the other. It's the closest thing there is to dancing on snow.

Once the leg motion is under control, it's time to add the pole action. Just as in downhill skiing, the pole acts as an imaginary pivot around which the turn is made. Thus for a right turn, the right pole is "planted"; likewise for a turn to the left. Telemark turns are somewhat tipsy from side to side, and at first the natural tendency is to hold one's arms high and out to the sides like a wire walker. Try to keep your arms low. That will help keep your center of gravity down—a more stable position. A final word of caution on downhills: Before descending through the trees, slip your hands out of your pole straps. It's far better to have to climb back uphill for a dropped pole than an arm!

Telemarking in the Gulf of Slides, NH.

Some of the most frequent mistakes made by beginners in learning to telemark include:

Holding back, that is, failing to commit enough weight to that leading ski. You've gotta believe! Your weight should be fairly evenly distributed between both skis.

Trying to angle the front ski too sharply, making it skid. To make a sharper turn, drop more deeply into the telemark position and lean into the turn harder.

Weighting the leading ski too early, causing it to get "stuck" in a groove.

Spreading one's legs too far apart or not weighting the tail ski enough, and crossing the trailing ski over the top of the leading one. This happens to everyone from time to time and, with practice, one can complete such a turn, the infamous "crossover telly."

Standing up too soon, before the turn is completed.

And last but not least, one error some skiers make is in taking this all far too seriously. After all, we've gone out to the backcountry to get away from the pressure to perform and be perfect, have we not? If we wanted perfect turns every time, we'd stick to the manicured slopes. Part of the beauty of backcountry adventure is learning to accept what Nature brings forth.

ICE AXES

"What on earth would I want one of those pointy things for?" is a question frequently asked by beginning winter hikers. "It looks like something used on Mary, Queen of Scots!" Indeed, for many backpackers who stick to the more gentle, well established trails an ice ax may be overkill. But for those who wish to climb to some of the steeper, craggier summits or travel in safety on the ice-plated areas above treeline, it will prove a valuable aid.

Each of those imposing points on the ax has a name. At the top of the ax is, naturally, its head, which is made up of the pick and a broader, flat adz. Woodworking buffs know that an adz is a tool used for squaring off logs into beams. The adz of an ice ax is used similarly, for carving out holds in the ice or hard snow. With advances in crampons and ice axes over the past thirty to forty years, the adz is seldom used for "chopping steps," although it

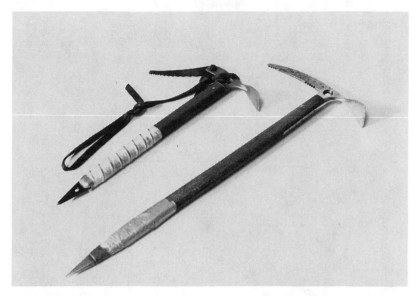

An ice climber's ax (left) with its steeply drooped pick, wrist loop, and very short handle, shown next to a more traditional hiking/mountaineering ax.

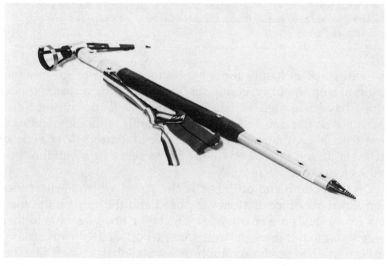

An ax with an adjustable handle.

*When it's not being used, the ice ax may be fastened to the pack by the "ice axes loop"
and a strap (a), or (b) by simply slipping it down between your pack and your
shoulderblades.*

may still come in handy for a very short stretch of ice to avoid
having to stop to put on crampons, or for leveling a sleeping platform. I have also seen an adz work very well for cutting blow-
downs across the trail and for slicing salamis, although neither of
these uses is recommended by the manufacturers. The pick, of
course, is driven into the snow or ice to serve as a handhold, or
used as a brake for self-arrest.

On the bottom end of the ax is the spike, which is sharpened
to grip in snow or ice. Between the head and the spike is the shaft.
Most ice ax shafts are now made of metal or fiberglass due to their
strength, although there are still some wood-shafted axes around.
For light-use hiking and scrambling a wood-shafted ax is fine, but
for more difficult climbing the synthetics are preferred. For general
hiking use, the shaft of the ax should be long enough to perform
a self-arrest, but not so long as to become unwieldy for ascending

If the snow is soft, the shaft of the ax can be plunged in so the climber can pull up on it.

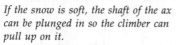

As the slope steepens, the ax can be held as a sort of diagonal brace (a). A somewhat unorthodox but very practical use of the ice ax on steep, wooded eastern trails is to hook the pick around a tree and pull (b).

a slope. Remember that the ax is much more than a walking stick; if this is all that's needed the winter hiker will probably be better served by a ski pole. For most winter hikers a 60–75 cm ax works out best. Those doing very steep or technical climbing will use shorter axes, from 70 cm down to hammer length. There are even some ice axes made that can be adjusted for length, although they are somewhat heavy and don't seem to have caught on yet.

For carrying the ax there are a number of rubber or leather guards available, but none of them is a substitute for being careful and most of them end up lost or thrown away after a year or two. On the approach to a climb, many people will fasten the ax to their packs using the "ice ax loop" at the bottom of the pack, but this places the spike in a somewhat dangerous position for anyone walking behind. Another option is to slip the ax, spike down, between your pack and your shoulderblades. This makes it readily available but has the disadvantage of placing the head of the ax close to one's own head, and there is some potential for injury should the climber take a spill. (Although I have never heard of this happening, most of the climbers who've had this happen can't quite remember it....) While carrying the ax by hand when it's not being used, be sure to maintain control of it at all times so that in the event of a fall it won't go flailing around and catch an unsuspecting companion in the teeth. Whether you carry it with the spike pointing forwards or backwards is the subject of considerable controversy among groups of people who seem to spend more time arguing about things like this than actually getting outside. When the going is very steep and there's a chance that a dropped ax will take a long ride, many climbers attach it to themselves by a wrist loop. The only problem with this is if the climber falls and lets go of the ax, the wrist loop may return it none too gently.

For climbing up with the ax it can be held in a number of ways, most of which have fancy French names. On nearly level terrain it can be held like a walking stick. Whether the pick is held forwards or backwards has also been the subject of some debate, by some of the same people in the spike forwards or backwards battle. The argument for holding the pick backwards is that it puts it in a better position for self arrest. The arguments for holding the pick forwards are: it's more comfortable, it points away from the climber and is therefore safer in the event of a stumble, and it's the way the French guides do it. Take your pick (sorry about that!).

As the slope angle steepens, the ax can be used as a sort of diagonal brace or, if the snow is soft, the shaft of the ax can be plunged in so the climber can then pull up on it. While traversing a slope or climbing diagonally upward, the ax should be held in the climber's uphill hand with the pick facing backward so that it will be in good position for a self arrest if it's needed. On the steepest of slopes the climber faces inward and drives the pick of the ax into the snow or ice and then climbs up by pulling down and slightly outwards on the shaft.

For descending, most of the same techniques can be reversed, including placing the pick in the slope and holding onto the shaft as if it were a banister.

Self-Arrest

The first thing to realize about self-arrest is that it's not what you do if you've committed a crime and feel guilty. The next thing to know is that it can't be learned from a book—it must be repeated until it becomes instinctive and then should be practiced regularly. It not only can save your life in the event of a fall, but when climbing as a roped team it may save the life of a partner.

The following description should give the reader a basic understanding of the technique. Before attempting to practice self-arrest, be sure that the practice slope has a safe runout free of rocks, trees, and other obstacles (dumpsters, wood chippers, etc.) in case anyone fails to stop, and check your insurance policy. Actually this is not as funny as it sounds. I once had a disability insurance policy that refused to cover me if I got hurt mountain climbing. I guess it was only for shuffleboard injuries and paper cuts. The first thing to learn is the "self-arrest position"; then one must learn how to get into that position from any possible fall. As shown in the photo, the ax is held in a cross-chest position with the spike by one hip and the head by the climber's opposite shoulder, with the pick directed into the snow, to be dragged as a brake. If the arrest is applied as soon as the climber falls, the pick can be quickly jammed into the snow surface. But if the climber is sliding with any speed it will be necessary to ease the pick in gradually. Otherwise it may be suddenly ripped from one's grasp. Once the pick has been set in the snow the climber must then maximize the braking force by bearing down on the head of the ax with her shoulders and chest, forming a tripod between her feet and the pick of the ax, with her hips held out away from the slope. If crampons are being worn, they can easily snag on the snow, causing a sprained ankle or worse, so the climber must lift her feet off the slope and brake with her knees instead. While practicing it's a good idea to pretend that you're wearing crampons while not actually using them.

This all assumes that one has fallen feet first, facing the snow, but it doesn't always happen that way. The other basic positions to practice are feet-first facing out, and head first, both facing in and facing out. To convert these positions into the basic self-arrest position the pick of the ax is used as a pivot to swing one's legs downhill, and then the climber rolls toward the pick to get on top of the ax. Rolling toward the spike can cause it to catch in the snow and flip the ax out of one's hands.

a

Maintenance

An all-metal or metal-fiberglass ax needs little maintenance except for an occasional coat of light oil to prevent rusting, and periodic sharpening, depending on how it's being used. Technical climbers may touch up their axes before every climb, while hikers may only

b

c

Ice ax self-arrest beginning in a face up, feet downhill position (a, b, c).

When crampons are worn, this position should be used to self-arrest, to prevent ankle injuries.

sharpen theirs once a season, if at all. Just as in woodcutting, though, a dull ax can be more dangerous than a sharp one, because it glances off the surface against which it's struck and it doesn't stick properly when it's needed. All sharpening should be done by hand with a file or an ax stone. High speed grinding wheels can easily overheat the metal and weaken it. Axes with wooden shafts should also receive an annual coating of linseed oil. Treat your ax right and it will be your friend for a lifetime.

Self-arrest from a head down position requires using the ax pick as a pivot to allow the climber to swing her legs downhill (a, b, c). From the position shown in (d), the climber must first roll over, and then continue as in (a) through (c).

CRAMPONS AND CREEPERS

Buying your first pair of crampons is thrilling, whether it stirs up visions of wandering surefooted around rime-coated sculptures at treeline, scaling vertical ice, or just negotiating a slippery spot on the trail. I bought my first pair en route to a week-long climbing trip. Fortunately my partner knew what to look for as I drooled at all the available models, and I ended up with a workable pair.

Types of Crampons

Crampons are either hinged in the middle or rigid throughout, and most have twelve or more points. Rigid crampons must be worn on rigid boots or else they will eventually break, whereas hinged or flexible crampons can be worn on either stiff or soft boots. Rigid

From left: hinged crampon with traditional bindings, hinged crampon with step-in binding, rigid crampon with step-in binding.

*Lacing a traditional crampon binding—
there should be no extra twists or slack
in the straps.*

crampons are preferred for difficult technical climbing because they penetrate ice more securely and are less tiring to the foot and calf muscles for long steep sections. For general hiking use up to and including moderate ice climbing, hinged crampons are fine. On most modern crampons there are two "front points" that enable the climber to balance on his or her toes for very steep sections. For hikers who don't plan to technical climb, the disadvantage of having those two points sticking out in front is they can catch on one's gaiters or windpants or, worse but uncommon, stick into the climber himself or one of his partners. One solution for those who don't plan to be doing any steep climbing is to tape over the front points.

Bindings and Adjustments

Once your new toys are out of their box the first thing to do is adjust them to fit your boots. This is usually done by changing the position of several small bolts or screws. Notice that some models have a definite left and right crampon. The vertical posts should fit

Always keep your crampons flat on the surface, so all points penetrate evenly.

Avoid edging, as this can cause the points to shear out of the ice.

As the grade steepens (a), one will need to turn more and more sideways. On the steepest of slopes (b), the climber faces inwards and uses just the two front points of his crampons.

snugly against the boot sole so the crampons will hang in place even before the bindings are fastened. Heating and bending the posts to improve the fit is done occasionally but it can weaken the metal. It's best to buy a crampon that fits your boot right from the start. There is often a stiff wire "bail" connecting the two rear posts which helps hold the boot heel in place. These can easily be improvised from stiff coathanger wire for crampons that lack them, and they are especially useful for the softer or narrower types of boots. It's a good idea to recheck the crampon fit before every trip. Screws and bolts can loosen, and if you use more than one pair of winter boots you'll want to be sure they're not adjusted for the other pair.

Crampon bindings generally consist of either a set of neoprene straps (traditional) or a metal bail in the front for the toe and a clamp on the back ("step-in" variety). For rigid boots the step-ins are faster and, if properly fitted (pay special attention to the toe section), very secure. For softer boots it is usually necessary to use the traditional bindings as the step-in mechanisms require a rigid boot to stay tight. With the strap-on types of bindings there are usually two straps per crampon, one that passes around the ankle and another that weaves back and forth across the forefoot. A recommended variant known as the "Scottish" type has two straps for the forefoot, one of which is fixed in position like a toe bail with a ring in the middle, through which the other strap is passed. This system cuts down on the amount of threading needed once the boot is positioned, thereby making attachment faster and easier. These straps sometimes come extra long and need to be cut down to size, and often need extra holes punched. Such tasks are far easier to do at home than with cold fingers and a dull pocketknife. Leave several inches of leeway to allow for different sock, boot, or gaiter combinations, but not so much that the straps drag on the ground, inviting a fall. They should fit as tightly as possible without cutting off circulation to the toes.

Using Crampons

There are a number of excellent books on the subject of ice ax and crampon use (see references), but a few basic points bear mentioning here. Walking with crampons on is fairly natural, but you must be careful to pick up your feet enough so the points don't catch and cause a stumble. Mountaineering literature is full of accounts of weary climbers descending and catching a crampon point during a moment of inattention. When crossing over rocky sections one must also take care not to step down hard on the relatively fragile connecting rod that holds the two halves of a hinged crampon together.

As the slope begins to steepen it becomes increasingly important to keep the points of the crampons flat on the surface. This is especially tough for skiers whose natural tendency is to edge on a slope, but edging with crampons will cause the points to shear out of the ice. On moderate slopes a splay-footed or herringbone step will be enough to keep the points in good contact with the surface, but as the grade steepens one will need to turn more and more sideways. On the steepest of slopes that can be climbed with this "French technique" (about 45° for most people) one ends up nearly backing up the slope. Anything too steep to be climbed by the French technique usually requires using the front two points of the crampons, known as "front-pointing." For a good description of this and other advanced techniques consult Yvon Chouinard's classic text, *Climbing Ice*.

Many of the same steps can be reversed to descend. In some cases, though, it's easiest to face out and head straight down, sitting back slightly and "slapping" the soles of your boots down hard on the ice. Because of its resemblance to the way a duck walks, the French refer to this way of descending as "en canard." I personally have never seen a duck wearing crampons; their feet are too wide. Now loons, that's a different story....

Jeepers, Creepers!

For an occasional short patch of ice, short crampons that go just under the middle part of the foot, known as "instep crampons" or "creepers," may be adequate, thus avoiding the weight and expense of regular crampons. For longer distances though, many people find that wearing instep crampons is like walking on blocks of wood, and whenever one's weight comes down on just the heel or the toe the creeper may slip and can cause some spectacular tumbles. As with any important piece of equipment, it's a good idea to rent or borrow both instep and regular crampons and test them out before buying any.

Sleds and Pulks

Sleds, pulks, and toboggans can make the work of hauling heavy supplies in to a base camp delightfully easy, or they can be an exercise in frustration. Sleds work best on fairly smooth, level and well-packed trails, such as abandoned roads or railroad beds, or on open snowfields or glaciers. On steep and rocky trails frequent tipping of the sled or catching on objects can make them more trouble than they're worth.

There are a number of companies and individuals who make excellent sleds with covers, compartments, runners, rigid harnesses, etc., but for occasional use one can often get by with a child's plastic sled from the hardware store and a few modifications. The first thing to do is remove the flimsy plastic handles and replace them with sturdy nylon cord, to which the load will be tied. Another useful modification is to bolt a piece of angle aluminum or two to the bottom of the sled to act as a runner and help keep it tracking straight. This is particularly useful on sidehills, one of the more difficult types of sledding terrain.

Unless one person is planning to follow behind the sled to keep it from sliding into the leader on downhills, one may want to consider towing it with some sort of springy steel or fiberglass wands rather than a rope to maintain the proper distance between the puller and the load. A cheap and effective alternative can be made by threading a rope through two four to six foot sections of ¾" PVC piping. This is especially helpful for skiers, to keep the sled from running up onto the tails of their skis. The downside of wands is that in difficult terrain such as trails with many bends or obstacles the wands may make it more difficult to maneuver, and one may be better off with a simple towrope. In this case when the load reaches the top of a hill the hauler can flip the rope up over the load and hold it back from behind like a farmer working a draft horse. With practice this transition from *puller* to *pullee* can go quickly and smoothly. When using wands one will need some sort of waist or chest harness, either bought or homemade (an old climbing harness works well), or one can clip them directly to the waist belt of a pack. Note that it is sometimes helpful to carry a small daypack in addition to the sled. This makes it easier to gain access to oft-needed items such as extra clothing and food, and in terrain with many steep uphills it is often easier to have some of the weight on one's back. Try to keep the load's center of gravity as low as possible by spreading the load out the whole length of the sled and putting heavier items on the bottom.

Sleds can also be used to evacuate an injured person or bring a small child along for the ride. For many families with small children who want to go winter camping, a sturdy sled is *the* way to go.

CARL E. HEILMAN II

Afterword

I was walking through Smugglers' Notch the other day when I met a hiker coming out of the woods. "I just came down off of the ridge," he recounted. "The last time I tried to do that I got lost, so this time I put up survey markers on the trees. That will help other people find their way out." I looked at him with a mixture of sadness and anger. I wanted to shout at him, "What right do you have to go marking up the woods with pieces of plastic? Don't you think if people choose to bushwhack they should be able to find their own way? And what about the impact of all of your followers crashing through the trees in the same spot?" But I didn't. Instead I tried to steer him gently into a conversation about bushwhacking, about the spirit of wilderness, about stewardship. In the end, I'm sorry to say, I'm not sure he got it. "Nobody goes up there anyways," he retorted, shaking his head. So I'm urging you, readers of this book, to give me a hand. As more and more people visit the backcountry in winter it becomes obvious that our wilderness on Earth is limited. I hope that the material presented here will help you enjoy the winter wilderness safely, and love it more with each new experience. If we all work together on preserving this critical resource, perhaps the next time I see that hiker up in the Notch he'll be gathering up bits of orange ribbon. I thank you in advance for your efforts, and wish you many years of winter enjoyment.

Please let me know if you have any suggestions to make this a better book. This may include tips on new pieces of equipment (don't hesitate to send samples!) as well as comments on other parts of the text. We are always learning in this game, myself included. Write me care of the Adirondack Mountain Club. Thanks.

John Dunn
Jeffersonville, VT
September 1996

Appendix

Recommended Supplies for Winter Backpacking

Food and Drink

Ample foodstuffs for duration of trip, plus at least one extra day's emergency rations

Stove with fuel, spare parts, repair tools, and stable, heat resistant base

Waterproof matches and fire starters

Cookware

Large, stable cup and/or bowl or deep dish

Spoon, fork, and other utensils as needed

Insulated water bottles and/or thermos

Clothing

Socks and underwear

Hat

Shirt and pants

Pile jacket or sweater

Bulky parka

Shell jacket and pants

Mittens or gloves, with overmitts

Boots

Gaiters, supergaiters, or overboots

Optional: vapor barrier liners, facemask, scarf, headband, earmuffs, pile pants, booties

Shelter and Sleeping

Sleeping bag

Foam pad, with or without air mattress

Tent

Optional: liner bag or overbag, snow saw and shovel, whisk broom to brush snow from clothing or tent

Other equipment

Skis or snowshoes with traction device, spare ski tip, waxes and/or climbing skins

Backpack

Headlamp or flashlight, with spare batteries and bulb

Knife

Sunglasses or goggles

Repair kit

First-aid kit

Map and compass

Toilet articles

Emergency kit, including whistle and/or signaling mirror

Optional: sled or pulk, ice ax, crampons or creepers, avalanche probes, cords or beepers, alarm clock or watch

References

General Hiking and Camping

Fletcher, Colin. *The Complete Walker III.* Alfred A. Knopf, Inc., NY. 1984.

Gorman, Stephen. *AMC Guide to Winter Camping.* AMC Books, Boston, 1991.

Manning, Harvey. *Backpacking, One Step at a Time.* Vintage Books, NY. 1980.

Peters, Ed (editor). *Mountaineering, the Freedom of the Hills.* The Mountaineers, Seattle, WA. 5th edition, 1992.

Hiking and Climbing History

Carson, Russell M.L. *Peaks and People of the Adirondacks.* Adirondack Mtn. Club, Glens Falls, NY. 1986.

Crawford, Lucy. *Lucy Crawford's History of the White Mountains.* Appalachian Mtn. Club, Boston, 1978.

Waterman, Guy and Laura. *Forest and Crag.* Appalachian Mtn. Club, Boston, 1989.

Waterman, Guy and Laura. *Yankee Rock and Ice.* Stackpole Books, Harrisburg, PA. 1993.

Conditioning

Hurn, Martyn and Ingle, Pat. *Climbing Fit.* The Crowood Press, Wiltshire, England 1988.

Kisner, Carolyn and Colby, Lynn. *Therapeutic Exercise: Foundations and Techniques.* F. A. Davis Co., Philadelphia, 1985.

Flora and Fauna

Ketchledge, E.H. *Forests and Trees of the Adirondack High Peaks Region*. Adirondack Mtn. Club, Lake George, NY. 1996.

Marchand, Peter J. *Life in the Cold*. Hanover and London, University Press of New England, 1987.

Murie, Olaus. *A Field Guide to Animal Tracks*. Houghton Mifflin Co. Boston, 1980.

Stokes, Donald W. *A Guide to Nature in Winter*. Little, Brown & Co. Boston, 1976.

Environmental Concerns

Nash, Roderick. *Wilderness and the American Mind*. New Haven and London: Yale University Press, 1973.

Waterman, Laura and Guy. *Backwoods Ethics: Environmental Issues for Hikers and Campers*. Countryman Press, Woodstock, VT. 1993.

Waterman, Laura and Guy. *Wilderness Ethics: Preserving the Spirit of Wilderness*. Countryman Press, Woodstock, VT. 1993.

Food and Drink

Barker, Harriett. *The One-Burner Gourmet*. Contemporary Books Inc., Chicago, 1981.

Fleming, June. *The Well-Fed Backpacker*. Vintage Books, NY. 3rd. ed. 1986.

Prater, Yvonne and Mendenhall, Ruth Dyer. *Gorp, Glop and Glue Stew*. The Mountaineers, Seattle. 1982.

Sukey, R. et al. *The NOLS Cookery*. NOLS and Stackpole Books, 3rd ed. 1991.

Snowshoeing

Osgood, Wm. and Hurley, Leslie. *The Snowshoe Book*. Stephen Greene Press, Brattleboro, VT. 3rd. ed. 1983.

Prater, Gene. *Snowshoeing*. The Mountaineers, Seattle, 1988.

Skiing

Barnett, Steve. *Cross-Country Downhill and other Nordic Mountain Skiing Techniques*. Globe Pequot Press, Chester, CT 1983.

Gillette, Ned and Dostal, John. *Cross-Country Skiing*. The Mountaineers, Seattle. 2nd. ed. 1988.

Goodman, David. *Classic Backcountry Skiing.* Boston: Appalachian Mountain Club, 1989.

Tejada-Flores, Lito. *Backcountry Skiing: The Sierra Club Guide to Skiing off the Beaten Track.* Sierra Club, San Francisco, 1981.

Routefinding and Navigation

Kjellstrom, Bjorn. *Be Expert with Map and Compass.* Charles Scribner's Sons, NY. 1976.

Randall, Glenn. *The Outward Bound Map & Compass Handbook.* New York: Lyons and Burford, 1987.

Rutsrum, Calvin. *The Wilderness Route Finder.* The MacMillan Co., NY. 1974.

Safety and First Aid

American Alpine Club. "Accidents in North American Mountaineering" (annual report)

Auerbach, Paul, MD. *Medicine for the Outdoors.* Little, Brown and Co. Boston/Toronto, 1986.

Daffern, Tony. *Avalanche Safety for Skiers and Climbers.* Alpenbooks, Seattle. 1983.

Forgey, Wm., MD. *Hypothermia: Death by Exposure.* ICS Books, 1985.

LaChapelle, Edward. *The ABC's of Avalanche Safety.* The Mountaineers, Seattle, 1978.

Setnicka, Tim J. *Wilderness Search and Rescue.* AMC Press, Boston, 1980.

Tilton, Buck, and Frank Hubbell. *Medicine for the Backcountry.* Merrillville, IN: ICS Books, 1990.

Wilkerson, James, MD (ed.) *Hypothermia, Frostbite and Other Cold Injuries.* The Mountaineers, Seattle, 1986.

About the Author

John Dunn grew up in New England and has been winter hiking and skiing for most of his life. He has worked several seasons for the Appalachian Mountain Club, where he was involved in numerous rescue operations, and has taught mountaineering for the ADK/AMC Winter Mountaineering School. Between backpacking trips he managed to finish medical school and spent three months in Nepal caring for sick and injured trekkers (as well as sneaking in a little climbing on the side). Beyond the Northeast and Nepal, he has also hiked and/or skied in the Rockies, the Pacific Northwest, Europe, New Zealand, and Mexico. Dunn has settled in Jeffersonville, Vermont where he divides his time between family, emergency medicine, writing, and enjoying the mountains.

Index

Working for wilderness and loving it.

JOIN US!

We are a nonprofit membership organization that brings together people with interests in recreation, conservation, and environmental education in the New York State Forest Preserve. Our 22,000 members pursue a wide range of outdoor activities, including hiking, canoeing, backpacking, climbing, skiing, and snowshoeing. Many also join ADK to support our work on trails and in the halls of government, and thus lend their voices to protecting New York's Adirondack and Catskill Parks.

Other benefits include:
* receipt of *Adirondac* six times per year
* discounts on ADK publications, educational workshops, and wilderness lodges
* the opportunity to join a local chapter and enjoy its outings and activities
* the opportunity to apply for the ADK Visa card

BACKCOUNTRY EDUCATION & STEWARDSHIP

ADK is a leader in teaching outdoor skills and promoting recreational activities consistent with the region's wild character. Thus the Club offers workshops ranging from field natural history to hiking, canoeing, and skiing, and orienteering and wilderness first aid.

In addition, ADKers are known for "giving back" to the places that have nurtured them, by participating in extensive work on trails throughout the New York State Forest Preserve.

For more information about the Adirondacks or about ADK:
Information Center & Headquarters
814 Goggins Road, Lake George, NY 12845-4117
518/668-4447
Exit 21 off I-87 ("the Northway"), 9N south

May–Columbus Day: Tues. after Columbus Day–May:
Mon.–Sat., 8:30 a.m.–5 p.m.   Mon.-Fri., 8:30 a.m.–4:30 p.m.

For lodge, cabin, or campground reservations on ADK's Heart Lake property in the High Peaks region, write or call:
Adirondack Mountain Club
Box 867
Lake Placid, NY 12946-0867
518/523-3441
(9 a.m.–7 p.m. daily)

To join ADK by credit card, please call our toll-free number: 800-395-8080 (8:30 a.m.–4:30 p.m., M–F). Callers who join may take immediate discount on ADK publications, workshops, and lodge stays and may charge all to VISA, MasterCard or Discover.

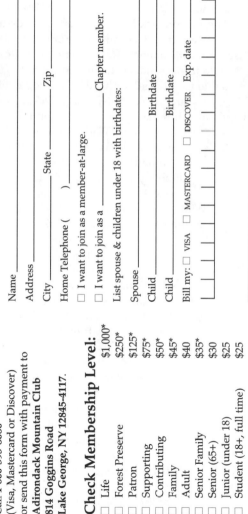

Membership

Adirondack ADK Mountain Club

To Join:

Call **1-800-395-8080**
(Visa, Mastercard or Discover)
or send this form with payment to
Adirondack Mountain Club
814 Goggins Road
Lake George, NY 12845-4117.

Check Membership Level:

☐ Life $1,000*
☐ Forest Preserve $250*
☐ Patron $125*
☐ Supporting $75*
☐ Contributing $50*
☐ Family $45*
☐ Adult $40
☐ Senior Family $35*
☐ Senior (65+) $30
☐ Junior (under 18) $25
☐ Student (18+, full time) ... $25

School _____

Includes associate/family members

All fees subject to change.

Name _____

Address _____

City _____ State _____ Zip _____

Home Telephone (___) _____

☐ I want to join as a member-at-large.

☐ I want to join as a _____ Chapter member.

List spouse & children under 18 with birthdates:

Spouse _____

Child _____ Birthdate _____

Child _____ Birthdate _____

Bill my: ☐ VISA ☐ MASTERCARD ☐ DISCOVER Exp. date _____

_____
Signature (required for charge)

ADK is a non-profit, tax-exempt organization. Membership fees are tax deductible, as allowed by law. Please allow 6-8 weeks for receipt of first issue of *Adirondac*.

WIN

The Adirondack Mountain Club, Inc.
814 Goggins Road
Lake George, NY 12845-4117
(518) 668-4447 / To order: 800-395-8080

BOOKS

An Adirondack Sampler I, Day Hikes for All Seasons
An Adirondack Sampler II, Backpacking Trips
Adirondack Canoe Waters: North Flow
Adirondack Canoe Waters: South & West Flow
The Adirondack Mt. Club Canoe Guide to
Western & Central New York State
Guide to Adirondack Trails: High Peaks Region
Guide to Adirondack Trails: Northern Region
Guide to Adirondack Trails: Central Region
Guide to Adirondack Trails: Northville–Placid Trail
Guide to Adirondack Trails: West-Central Region
Guide to Adirondack Trails: Eastern Region
Guide to Adirondack Trails: Southern Region
Guide to Catskill Trails
Climbing in the Adirondacks
Classic Adirondack Ski Tours
Winterwise: A Backpacker's Guide
Adirondack Park Mountain Bike Book
85 Acres: A Field Guide to the Adirondack Alpine Summits
Forests & Trees of the Adirondack High Peaks Region
Geology of the Adirondack High Peaks Region
Adirondack Wildguide (distributed by ADK)
The Adirondack Reader
Our Wilderness: How the People of New York Found, Changed, and
Preserved the Adirondacks

MAPS

Trails of the Adirondack High Peaks Region
Trails of the Northern Region
Trails of the Central Region
Northville–Placid Trail
Trails of the West-Central Region
Trails of the Eastern Region
Trails of the Southern Region

Price list available on request.